3/2000

Eating Disorders

OTHER BOOKS OF RELATED INTEREST

Eating Disorders

Myra H. Immell, *Book Editor*

David L. Bender, *Publisher*
Bruno Leone, *Executive Editor*
Bonnie Szumski, *Editorial Director*
Brenda Stalcup, *Managing Editor*
Scott Barbour, *Senior Editor*

Contemporary Issues
Companion

Greenhaven Press, Inc., San Diego, CA

Every effort has been made to trace the owners of copyrighted material. The articles in this volume may have been edited for content, length, and/or reading level. The titles have been changed to enhance the editorial purpose. Those interested in locating the original source will find the complete citation on the first page of each article.

No part of this book may be reproduced or used in any form or by any means, electrical, mechanical, or otherwise, including, but not limited to, photocopy, recording, or any information storage and retrieval system, without prior written permission from the publisher.

Library of Congress Cataloging-in-Publication Data

Eating disorders / Myra H. Immell, book editor.
    p.   cm. — (Contemporary issues companion)
  Includes bibliographical references and index.
  ISBN 1-56510-895-7 (lib. : alk. paper). —
ISBN 1-56510-894-9 (pbk. : alk. paper)
  1. Eating disorders. I. Immell, Myra. II. Series (Unnumbered)
RC552.E18I46 1999
616.85'26—dc21   98-35418
                                                           CIP

CONTENTS

FOREWORD

In the news, on the streets, and in neighborhoods, individuals are confronted with a variety of social problems. Such problems may affect people directly: A young woman may struggle with depression, suspect a friend of having bulimia, or watch a loved one battle cancer. And even the issues that do not directly affect her private life—such as religious cults, domestic violence, or legalized gambling—still impact the larger society in which she lives. Discovering and analyzing the complexities of issues that encompass communal and societal realms as well as the world of personal experience is a valuable educational goal in the modern world.

Effectively addressing social problems requires familiarity with a constantly changing stream of data. Becoming well informed about today's controversies is an intricate process that often involves reading myriad primary and secondary sources, analyzing political debates, weighing various experts' opinions—even listening to firsthand accounts of those directly affected by the issue. For students and general observers, this can be a daunting task because of the sheer volume of information available in books, periodicals, on the evening news, and on the Internet. Researching the consequences of legalized gambling, for example, might entail sifting through congressional testimony on gambling's societal effects, examining private studies on Indian gaming, perusing numerous websites devoted to Internet betting, and reading essays written by lottery winners as well as interviews with recovering compulsive gamblers. Obtaining valuable information can be time-consuming—since it often requires researchers to pore over numerous documents and commentaries before discovering a source relevant to their particular investigation.

Greenhaven's Contemporary Issues Companion series seeks to assist this process of research by providing readers with useful and pertinent information about today's complex issues. Each volume in this anthology series focuses on a topic of current interest, presenting informative and thought-provoking selections written from a wide variety of viewpoints. The readings selected by the editors include such diverse sources as personal accounts and case studies, pertinent factual and statistical articles, and relevant commentaries and overviews. This diversity of sources and views, found in every Contemporary Issues Companion, offers readers a broad perspective in one convenient volume.

In addition, each title in the Contemporary Issues Companion series is designed especially for young adults. The selections included in every volume are chosen for their accessibility and are expertly edited in consideration of both the reading and comprehension levels of the audience. The structure of the anthologies also enhances accessibility. An introductory essay places each issue in context and provides helpful facts such as historical background or current statistics and legislation that pertain to the topic. The chapters that follow organize the material and focus on specific aspects of the book's topic. Every essay is introduced by a brief summary of its main points and biographical information about the author. These summaries aid in comprehension and can also serve to direct readers to material of immediate interest and need. Finally, a comprehensive index allows readers to efficiently scan and locate content.

The Contemporary Issues Companion series is an ideal launching point for research on a particular topic. Each anthology in the series is composed of readings taken from an extensive gamut of resources, including periodicals, newspapers, books, government documents, the publications of private and public organizations, and Internet websites. In these volumes, readers will find factual support suitable for use in reports, debates, speeches, and research papers. The anthologies also facilitate further research, featuring a book and periodical bibliography and a list of organizations to contact for additional information.

A perfect resource for both students and the general reader, Greenhaven's Contemporary Issues Companion series is sure to be a valued source of current, readable information on social problems that interest young adults. It is the editors' hope that readers will find the Contemporary Issues Companion series useful as a starting point to formulate their own opinions about and answers to the complex issues of the present day.

INTRODUCTION

"Well, I eat . . . when I'm hungry . . . when I'm full . . . when I'm anxious . . . when I'm happy . . . when I'm sad . . . well, you get the idea. Food, the friend that never fails," explains Tom, who is in his thirties. Mackenzie, a young woman in her twenties, is the direct opposite of Tom when it comes to food. "Kids pointed and sales clerks whispered as I stood in line with my children's size 10 dresses, but my embarrassment wasn't enough to quell the voice inside my head that taunted, You need to be smaller," Mackenzie confides. Then there is Michael, a teenager who admits, "I knew there was something wrong with what I was doing, but I couldn't stop. There were times I wished I could die, but still I couldn't make myself eat anything." Marya, another young woman in her twenties, was once given a week to live when her weight dropped to 52 pounds. "Faced with a choice—eat or die—I ate," states Marya. "It was not as easy a choice as one might expect." Marya and the others live in different parts of the United States. They are neither friends nor acquaintances. In fact, they have never met. Yet all four have something in common—they each struggle with an eating disorder.

Eating disorders include a range of conditions that "involve an obsession with food, weight and appearance to the degree that a person's health, relationships and daily activities are adversely affected," according to the Center for Eating Disorders. The three most common eating disorders are anorexia nervosa, bulimia nervosa, and binge eating disorder. Anorexia nervosa is characterized by self-starvation. Anorexics do not eat enough to maintain a healthy weight; they may also use vomiting, laxatives, diuretics, or exercise to control their weight. They may not admit—even to themselves—that their weight loss or restricted eating is a problem, and they often feel fat no matter how much weight they lose. Bulimia nervosa is characterized by binge eating and purging. Bulimics eat large amounts of high-calorie food in a short period of time, then vomit and/or use laxatives to rid their system of the food before their body absorbs it. Typically, bulimics realize that their behavior is not normal and feel guilt and shame over it, but they are unable to stop the binge-and-purge cycle. Binge eating disorder is also characterized by binge eating and/or continual overeating, but it does not involve purging. People with this disorder eat whether they are physically hungry or not.

Eating disorders generally are regarded as phenomena of the twentieth century. But some academics believe that these behaviors can be traced back to Medieval Europe and to the Victorian era in England and the United States. In modern times, eating disorders most often have been associated with females. Historically, however, one of the first cases of eating disorders ever documented was that of a male—a sixteen-year-old boy—reported in 1694 by London physician Richard Morton. "Abandon your Studies," Morton advised his patient, "go into the Country Air, use Riding, and a Milk Diet . . . for a long time." Treatment today is much more complex—hospitalizations, several years or more of therapy, medical monitoring, and medications. It also is expensive: $30,000 or more per month for inpatient treatment and as much as $100,000 or more for outpatient treatment over the long term.

Anorexia, bulimia, and binge eating disorder do not discriminate by gender or background. They affect both men and women of all age groups and of every racial and ethnic background. However, different ethnic groups do tend to exhibit certain eating disorders more than others. According to a 1998 Public Health Department report, Asian American high school women with eating disorders reported more binge eating, African Americans reported relatively higher rates of vomiting, and Hispanic females were more apt to use diuretics to control weight.

Two of the three most common eating disorders—anorexia nervosa and bulimia nervosa—are classified as mental illnesses. People with these disorders often have other mental disorders as well. In fact, experts conclude that the odds of having both an eating disorder and another mental illness may be as high as 50 percent.

The modern public became painfully aware of just how serious these disorders could be in the early 1980s when a popular female vocalist, Karen Carpenter, died from heart failure associated with anorexia nervosa. Current statistics are sobering. According to the National Association of Anorexia Nervosa and Associated Disorders, seven million females and one million males—children and adults—suffer from eating disorders. Experts agree that it is difficult to determine exactly how widespread the problem is because people often hide their symptoms or do not try to seek treatment or help. However, medical and clinical guidelines exist that may be used to help determine if someone has an eating disorder. When asked how to tell if someone might be suffering from an eating disorder, Joanna Moyer, director of Women's Health at Pennsylvania State University, offered this uncomplicated method: "When a person's life becomes centered around food, weight and exercise and when decisions are based on how much they have eaten, on what the scale says, or how much exercise they can fit in—an eating disorder may exist."

Medical authorities do not know to what extent physiological factors, psychological factors, or a combination of both cause the disorders. However, most experts agree that body image is an important aspect of eating disorders and that dieting behavior is almost always present in the development of an eating disorder. The U.S. Public Health Service's Office on Women's Health reports that the number of people in the United States affected by eating disorders has doubled between the 1970s and the 1990s. This increase may be connected to the fact that in the 1970s only 6 percent of teenagers worried about their weight, while in the 1990s, the number has grown to almost 40 percent. The relation between eating disorders and weight control has become a matter of concern among both health professionals and Americans in general. Many view society's emphasis on weight control, rather than weight control itself, as problematic. According to the National Women's Health Information Center, at any given time, 40 percent of American women are dieting even though half of them are at normal weight. One study of high school girls found that while 26 percent dieted, only 12 percent were actually overweight. Some experts warn that an overemphasis on dieting may make certain individuals more likely to develop an eating disorder.

Victims of eating disorders are among the first to admit that an eating disorder constitutes long-term suffering. Experts agree that there is no overnight cure and that, even with therapy, the risk of relapse is high. "Death rates from anorexia, bulimia, binge eating disorder and restrictive eating habits," states the U.S. Department of Public Health, "are among the highest for any mental illness." The National Institute of Mental Health reports that one in ten individuals with anorexia nervosa dies of starvation, cardiac arrest, or other medical complications.

While both body image and dieting are important aspects of eating disorders, clearly not everyone who diets or who is concerned about body image falls victim to a serious eating disorder like anorexia. That does not mean, however, that milder eating disturbances are not a matter of concern. According to the American Anorexia/Bulimia Association (AABA),

> Eating Disorders are not just the extremes of Anorexia Nervosa, Bulimia and Binge Eating Disorder. Dangerous eating and dieting practices, like the use of diet pills, laxatives and diuretics, and extreme fad diets, are widespread in this country. And, in a society obsessed with thinness as the surest sign of success, nearly every American man, woman and child has suffered at one time or another with issues of weight, body shape and self-image. The depression, shame and agonizing sense of isolation caused by Eating Disorders disrupts families, interrupts schooling, damages careers bright with promise and destroys relationships.

Increasingly, eating disorders have become regarded as a growing public health threat and, thus, an important government policy issue. At a 1997 congressional briefing cosponsored by the American Psychological Association, Representatives Louise M. Slaughter and Nita Lowey introduced the Eating Disorders Information and Education Act of 1997. The legislation, which became law in November 1997, established a program to provide information and education on the prevention and treatment of eating disorders.

The goal of the selections in *Eating Disorders: Contemporary Issues Companion* is much the same as that of the legislation—to provide information and insights on eating disorders. The selections cover a variety of topics and themes integral to understanding eating disorders, from symptoms to causes to the emotional, social, and physical impact of the disorders to treatment and recovery. The authors of the selections include health care professionals, people who suffer from have suffered from an eating disorder, and concerned family members or friends. The common denominator among them is a genuine concern about the dangers and pervasiveness of eating disorders.

CHAPTER 1

EATING DISORDERS: THE FACTS

EATING DISORDERS: AN OVERVIEW

Linda Ciotola

In the following selection, Linda Ciotola, a certified health education specialist and fitness instructor, provides an overview of three common eating disorders—anorexia, bulimia, and compulsive overeating. Ciotola explains that the causes of eating disorders are complex, involving biological, psychological, and social factors. She writes that eating disorders often result from attempts to regulate mood. For people with eating disorders, contends Ciotola, eating or dieting serves as a form of escape from emotional problems, such as low self-esteem. Among the broad range of behaviors Ciotola lists as exhibited by people with eating disorders are perfectionism, difficulty handling stress, distorted body image, and constant preoccupation with food, weight, body size, and shape.

Eating disorders result from a complicated interaction of biological, psychological, and social factors. People with eating disorders are intensely preoccupied with food, weight, and appearance, jeopardizing their health and adversely affecting relationships.

Although eating disorders most often affect adolescent females, they can affect children as well as older adults, males as well as females, across racial, ethnic, and socioeconomic lines. Some studies show that as many as 20% of eating disorder patients die as a result of their eating disorder.

Physical complications can affect the heart, blood pressure, the gastrointestinal system, teeth and gums, as well as the liver and kidney. Amenorrhea and malnutrition increase the risk of osteoporosis. Impaired concentration and thinking result from biochemical imbalances due to malnutrition, anemia, and fluctuating blood sugars. Compulsive over-eaters often suffer from heart disease, adult on-set diabetes, and other obesity-related health consequences.

While patients may layer clothes to hide the body shape underneath, many malnourished patients experience intense sensitivity to cold and/or heat due to a lowered core body temperature. Headaches, fatigue, weakness, dizziness, fainting, low energy, and decreased

Reprinted from Linda Ciotola, "Eating Disorders: An Overview of Anorexia, Bulimia, and Compulsive Overeating," http://www.doubleclickd.com/1expo96/source/eating.html (2/23/98), by permission of the author.

resistance to infection are also symptoms. Eating-disordered athletes may experience frequent orthopedic injuries due to compromised bone health and the effect of malnutrition on muscles and connective tissues.

Diet and Mood

Eating disorders often begin with diet. A person with low self-esteem attempts to feel better by dieting to look slimmer, perhaps in an attempt to conform to the current societal ideal (slender for women; lean and muscular for men). Sometimes dieting gets out of control and the dieter feels that "thin" is never thin enough and continues restricting food intake, firmly convinced that he/she is fat, even at low body weight.

Eating disorders are often an attempt to regulate mood. Ironically, acting on the eating disorder often has the opposite effect. Changes in brain biochemistry can intensify sleep and mood disturbances and appetite by dysregulation. Obsessive thoughts about food, weight, and appearance increase as the eating disorder intensifies. Further, persons with a family history of mood disorders, chemical dependency, and/or eating disorders appear to be a higher risk for the development of eating disorders. These suspected neurotransmitter dysregulations may be treated with anti-depressant and/or other appropriate medications.

Although medications can be helpful, they do have side effects and not all patients can tolerate them. Medications are not a cure because eating disorders result from a combination of bio-psycho-social factors which demand multi-disciplinary treatment. Even circadian and seasonal rhythms can affect brain biochemistry and it is possible that traditional Chinese acupuncture may be helpful in regulating these biochemicals and reducing cravings.

Behaviors and Characteristics

Many of the following behavioral characteristics have been observed among eating-disorder patients:

- Dieting, restricting, fasting
- Bingeing—a typical binge consists of 3,000 to 10,000 calories being ingested between 20–40 minutes
- Purging—by self-induced vomiting, laxative abuse, use of ipecac, diet pills, diuretics, and/or compulsive over-exercise
- Food rituals such as cutting and dicing food into small pieces, arranging food in a particular way on the plate, chewing a certain number of times before swallowing
- Collecting recipes, food coupons
- Obsessing, counting calories, fat grams
- Cooking and baking for others
- Discomfort when eating with others

- Secret hoarding and/or secretive eating of food
- Shoplifting, petty thievery (often to get food)
- Fear of inability to stop eating
- Constant preoccupation with food, weight, body size and shape
- Layered, loose fitting clothing
- Excessive activity, restlessness, insomnia, early morning awakening
- Chemical dependency
- Promiscuity—a reflection of poor impulse control sometimes seen in bulimic patients
- Obsessive-compulsive behaviors
- Isolation
- Suicide attempt
- People pleasing behavior, seeking external validation
- Poor impulse control
- Intense preoccupation with food, weight, appearance, image
- Intense fear of becoming "fat"
- Distorted body image (feeling fat when thin)
- Perfectionism
- Low self-esteem
- Lack of intimacy: issues of trust, honesty, and control
- Difficulty identifying and expressing feelings (calexthymia)
- Difficulty asking for help
- Irritability
- Difficulty concentrating
- Anxiety—difficulty handling stress
- Low frustration tolerance
- Dichotomous thinking ("all" or "nothing")

Anorexics usually deny having a problem, saying that everything is "under control" and claiming, "You're only trying to make me fat."

Bulimics and compulsive over-eaters, on the other hand, know their behavior is problematic but feel intense feelings of shame and guilt and may deny the behaviors in an attempt to maintain secrecy.

A Coping Mechanism

However, getting someone with an eating disorder to treatment is often difficult since persons act upon their eating disorders (restricting, bingeing, purging, etc.) as ways of dealing with emotional distress. Eating disorders are symptoms of underlying emotional distress, a way to numb or distract from underlying painful feelings.

Controlling food intake through eating disordered behavior is a maladaptive coping mechanism. Filling up with food may be an attempt to fill emotional needs.

In addition to individual personality and family dynamics, a correlation between emotional, physical, and sexual abuse and eating disorders has been established. These present a number of issues which must be addressed: fear of foods, body image distortions, problems with relationships, control, and trust, to name a few.

Socio-cultural influences are widespread and pervasive, and present an environment in which a person with low esteem could be encouraged to seek external validation by attempting to conform to unrealistic media images. Persons involved in a sport, art, or profession with emphasis on weight or appearance are a higher risk for development of eating disorders: models, gymnasts, divers, body builders, jockeys, wrestlers, distance runners, and ballet dancers, for example.

A Team Approach to Treatment

Since eating disorders are a complicated interplay of various factors, treatment necessitates a multi-disciplinary team approach: physician, therapist, nutritionist. In addition, expressive arts therapists and exercise specialists can be a valuable part of the treatment team. Clients need individual, group, expressive, cognitive, and family therapy; body image treatment, stress management; nutrition education and counseling and education. Confidential support groups are a helpful adjunct to treatment.

Individuals are encouraged to engage in treatment and to remain in treatment as long as necessary. Relapses are an expected part of recovery and clients are encouraged to ask themselves what's really bothering them when they feel like re-engaging in eating-disordered behaviors. This allows the relapse to become a learning experience.

Recovery from eating disorders is a long-term process, and while a small portion become chronic and still others struggle with periodic lapses, many persons do recover.

When Food Dominates

Tami J. Lyon

According to Tami J. Lyon, a registered dietician, food plays a major role in eating disorders. Lyon writes that the normal function of food is to nourish a person's body. However, she explains, people with eating disorders typically develop a new and abnormal set of rules applying to food that gradually dominates their lives. Not only do these rules signal an unhealthy obsession with food, she emphasizes, but they also lead to situations in which not enough nutrients and energy are consumed for good health. Instead, Lyon states, the extreme dieting or cycles of binging and purging associated with eating disorders cause malnutrition, which has serious physical and medical consequences.

Food is the vehicle of an eating disorder. Food influences your physical and mental health, and consequently, your very existence in the world. Food is vital to your recovery from an eating disorder.

Adequate nutrition allows your brain to think—to examine and understand both internal and external experiences. Adequate nourishment allows your body to perform vital processes for survival and health; however, in anorexia and bulimia, food moves beyond the role of nourishment for the body and becomes the object of rules, regulations and judgments that dominate one's life. The lack of food, via restrictive intake, purging, and/or excessive exercise, physiologically drives the mounting obsession with weight and body shape so characteristic of an eating disorder.

Let's look at the transition of the healthful use of food as nourishment to the painful use of food as a dominating force of esteem using a metaphor. As an eating disorder begins, so do food rules. The persistent, progressive evolution of "food rules" can be likened to the development of a large, complex computer file complete with a directory and subdirectories.

Rules are logged alphabetically in the directory. For example, all food rules related to fat can be found under "F" and in the subdirectory under "Fat." Initially, food, health, exercise, and weight beliefs did not require so much organization and memory. Simple, healthful guidelines easily fit in a small, basic file. There was no need

Abridged from Tami J. Lyon, "From Food as Nourishment to Food as Dominating Force," Optimal Eating website, http://www.healthyeating.com/tami.htm (3/22/98). Reprinted with permission from Optimal Eating.

for a directory or subdirectories. But, as an eating disorder develops, more rules and regulations about food, weight, and nutrition are written and enforced. All of these new rules require memory space and greater organization. The file becomes complex, demanding, and powerful. Other files that contained information about health, eating, weight, and exercise are deleted to accommodate the memory needed for this new file, the Eating Disorder. Files which contained information on interests outside food and eating are either shortened or deleted. This master file is stuffed with rules and guidelines about food, eating, exercise, and weight and continues to grow as the eating disorder develops and influences a person's life. If you are a person with an eating disorder, you may feel controlled by the rules contained in these files—they become your central rules for living, and it may feel as if you cannot live without them.

Dieting Above All

Through the new rules and regulations food takes on a different meaning. Foods you once enjoyed are now categorized as "bad" and only permitted in small quantities or not allowed at all. Guidelines from various diets you may have read about are merged, producing the strictest rules possible to lose weight or maintain a goal weight. Nutrition and health guidelines for the general public, delivered through the media and marketed by authors of diet books, are rigorously enforced as if they were written precisely for you. Frequently, they are enforced at a level several times beyond the general recommendation. The rules of the Eating Disorder file demand it.

Choices seem to disappear. Eating becomes rigid, limited, and a source of personal judgment and scorn. Every action must be in accord with the rules, which constantly up the ante for weight loss and discipline.

Many professionals believe that dieting is one entry path for an eating disorder. The impetus for dieting can come from a variety of events or situations, culminating in a desire to lose weight. An offhand, weight-related remark from a friend or a stranger, the break-up of a relationship, or the loss of a loved one can trigger the desire for weight loss in some individuals. Frequently, eating disorders begin during adolescence, when young women and men experience the changes of puberty in their bodies. These natural changes in body shape and composition are frequently viewed by young women as undesirable, and they feel out of control.

Women in our society experience cultural pressure to achieve an unrealistic, prepubescent, thin body shape and are encouraged to sculpt their bodies by any means possible to achieve this commercially promoted ideal. For some, dieting unleashes the Eating Disorder file, causing eating and weight to take on some new, unhealthful meanings.

Dietary Trends in Anorexia

Some research has been done on eating patterns in anorexia and bulimia. There is no exact eating pattern in any situation, but trends do emerge. In anorexia, there is an absolute reduction in caloric intake, many times accentuated by a significant increase in activity.

The primary dietary trends are the consumption of a low fat diet, vegetarianism and a preference toward or avoidance of sweets such as candy or frozen yogurt. Individual eating styles are unique, but what is universal, when evaluated alone or with energy expended through activity, is that the amount of energy consumed is inadequate for good health. Because overall food intake is low, intake of the macro-nutrients protein, fat, and carbohydrate suffers. Many times carbohydrate, found in vegetables, fruits, breads and cereals, etc. becomes the mainstay of the diet to the exclusion of protein and fat. Frequently, dietary intake of fat is drastically reduced. This reduction may emanate from the well-publicized emphasis on a low fat diet for good health and weight loss. However, the levels permitted by the Eating Disorder file are usually far below those recommended for good health.

Protein intake is also reduced, frequently to unhealthful levels. This reduction may occur as part of an individual's overall decrease in calories or protein may be specifically targeted for its supposed high fat content. This creates a deficit in the raw materials that the body needs to function.

Proteins which are found in meat, fish, poultry, eggs, cheese, milk, beans, and legumes are the building blocks of the body. Protein's primary role in the body is to repair and build new tissue. Skeletal muscle, hair, eyes, the immune system, heart, and skin are all made of protein. When dietary protein is inadequate, these tissues are not repaired and begin to break down (hair loss, weakened heart, brittle nails, for example). Inadequate fat intake also has its consequences. It can lead to poor absorption of fat soluble vitamins such as vitamins E, D, and A, cold intolerance, dry skin, loss of menstrual function, and even a clinical deficiency of essential fatty acids.

Dietary Trends in Bulimia

Dietary trends seen in bulimia include a number of different eating patterns. Similar to anorexia, there is a pattern of restricted food intake. Individuals may classify this minimal food intake as "good" and necessary to achieve or maintain a desired weight. In addition, there is binge eating, classically described as consuming a large quantity of food in a brief period of time.

Looking beyond the definition, a binge is a very subjective experience and can be defined in a number of ways: 1) eating more than allowed on the "good" plan, by a lot or very little, 2) eating in a very frenzied, "out of body" fashion, not tasting the food, just stuffing it down, or 3) eating a forbidden food (a food not allowed in the "good" diet). Binge eating can be spontaneous; a "good" meal goes too far: you begin eating and just can't stop, an unrestrainable hunger emerges. Or, binges can take on a life of their own; planned, guarded, feared, and relished. For some, every eating episode is a binge, and eating in control is no longer a possibility.

Purging, ridding the body of the unwanted food, is a component of bulimia. This may be accomplished through vomiting, laxatives, diet pills, exercise, or food restriction. Each of these purging methods affects the way the body functions and can be life threatening. Tangible problems such as electrolyte imbalance, cardiac arrhythmia, esophageal tears (leaving blood in vomit or stools), dehydration, colonic damage, etc. can and do occur from purging. Feeling like one's been hit by a Mack truck is a common sensation after a binge/purge episode. The body is reacting to receiving and losing (possibly violently) nutrients, water, and electrolytes. Individuals struggling with anorexia may also use binge eating and purging and experience negative physical effects.

Consequences of Eating Disorders

As you can see, eating disorders are not without consequences. Most of the physical consequences are related to malnutrition, starvation, and purging. Physically, you might notice hair loss (by the handful is not uncommon), bruises and cuts that do not heal, dry and cracked skin, fine downy hair on your face and arms, being cold (even on a warm, sunny day), dizziness when sitting up or standing, and extreme fatigue. These symptoms occur through a number of different pathways in the body, but the common cause is malnutrition. The body is not receiving enough nourishment to function; that means there are not enough calories, protein, fat, carbohydrates, vitamins, minerals, and fluids.

A medical clinician can assess additional parameters where eating patterns affect one's health. These may include pulse, blood pressure, and temperature. Blood tests that evaluate electrolyte and hormone levels may also be taken. And, if appropriate, bone scans may be completed to assess bone density. Individuals with eating disorders frequently have decreased pulse rates, low blood pressure (below a level that is healthy), and low body temperature. Tests of electrolytes and hormone levels may also come back abnormal.

Electrolyte imbalances resulting from starvation and/or purging play havoc with the body's ability to conduct electrical impulses. These impulses are the workhorses of basic bodily functions, such as heart beat. Women with anorexia and some women with bulimia lose their periods. For most, this is due to hormonal changes resulting from weight loss brought about by poor diet, and sometimes, by excessive exercise. Others may lose their periods prior to weight loss, due to chaotic and poor eating habits. To protect itself, the body makes hormonal changes which then can often put individuals with eating disorders at risk for losing bone density, which may not be recovered.

The Starving Body

There have been studies of what happens to the body when it does not get the energy and nutrients it needs to function, resulting in significant weight loss—it starves. An important note, significant weight loss does not have to occur for the body to be malnourished. Many individuals with bulimia, including those whose weight hasn't changed or has increased since the beginning of the eating disorder, are malnourished and may be at medical risk.

During starvation, the body must look to itself to supply the energy that is not being provided through food. The body uses stored carbohydrate and fat. But it does not use these alone. The body also goes to internal sources of protein, including skeletal muscle, heart tissue, and blood proteins for energy.

The body begins to break itself down to survive using a type of "cannibalism." There is a loss of lean tissue—skeletal muscle, for example—with any weight loss, but drastic reductions of energy intake result in much higher levels of lean tissue loss. As weight loss progresses, there is no carbohydrate or fat left to process, only lean, functional tissue, that which makes a person breathe, think, and move. This loss of protein affects the whole body, including the heart. The heart gets smaller and weaker and is not able to function very well. It becomes vulnerable to malfunctions, such as heart attacks.

The body will try to save itself from this "cannibalization" by reducing the metabolic rate, therefore reducing the amount of energy expended. This reduction in metabolic rate is reversed when adequate energy and nutrients are consumed in the diet. Serum cholesterol levels can be very low or high due to changes the body makes to survive starvation. An elevated cholesterol level in this situation does not warrant a low fat diet! Electrolyte imbalances can occur, especially if one vomits and/or uses laxatives. Initially, an eating disorder can cause your body systems to begin showing signs of stress (low blood pressure, pulse, and temperature); if unchecked, one's entire body system can fail (heart attack, kidney failure, death).

Effects of Malnutrition

Other changes associated with the malnutrition of eating disorders include early satiety (feeling full) and bloating due to delayed digestion in the stomach. You may experience decreased appetite for brief or extended periods of time due to increased levels of metabolites from an alternative energy pathway.

Sometimes, when you are in this state, eating will cause the lack of appetite to go away and an intense hunger may appear. The hunger is real, not a betrayal by your body. Actually, it is a much more accurate reflection of your body's nutritive state. Constipation can occur due to low calories and altered metabolic rate. In many cases, the small amount of food consumed does not provide enough bulk for normal bowel movements.

The malnutrition of an eating disorder also affects the way your brain functions. It may be more difficult to identify these changes, because in many ways they work with the eating disorder's rules and regulations. Behavioral changes seen in starvation and eating disorders include a preoccupation with food, binge eating or a loss of control when food is available, impaired concentration, indecisiveness, mood swings, depression, and social isolation. These consequences make it difficult to clearly assess what is going on, therefore enabling the eating disorder to thrive.

Nutrition and Recovery

Recovery can be a very difficult process, and understandably more than an individual can do on her or his own. Because an eating disorder is so pervasive, treatment usually includes a team of professionals so that each area of your life and health can be appropriately addressed. Nutrition is vital to recovery. Changing your diet by incorporating the energy, nutrients, and fluids necessary for proper brain, heart, and immune function makes it possible for you to become physically stronger. This strength enables you to move to a new place. A place, perhaps, where you can continue on a path leading to recovery. It is difficult, if not impossible, to think about such a process with a brain that isn't functioning well. The Eating Disorder file is running the show, and the weakened physical state frequently seen in eating disorders (even if you exercise a lot) makes it so difficult to make changes.

The good news is that much of the medical deterioration from an eating disorder is reversible with time and nutritional rehabilitation. This requires providing your body with the energy, nutrients, vitamins, minerals and fluid necessary to function. Nutritional recovery is not about excesses. It is not about "fattening up." Nutritional recovery is a progressive process where food, an element vital to life, is reintroduced in a fashion to promote your health and well-being.

AN UNHEALTHY OBSESSION

Frances M. Berg

Licensed nutritionist and family wellness specialist Frances M. Berg is an adjunct professor at the University of North Dakota School of Medicine and the author of eight books. In the following excerpt from her book *Afraid to Eat: Children and Teens in Weight Crisis*, Berg provides information and statistics about eating disorders, which have risen to crisis levels among children, teens, and young adults. Berg identifies and explains the causes, symptoms, and effects of such disorders as anorexia, bulimia, and binge eating disorder. She also explores the reasons why many experts consider dieting an important risk factor in developing eating disorders.

As American adults continue to obsess about weight and diet, it is hardly surprising that eating disorders among their children have risen to crisis levels.

While overweight may carry health risks over a lifetime, some eating disorders, like anorexia nervosa, can be deadly and take but a few years to kill.

Several estimates suggest the severity of these disorders. One textbook estimates that 10 to 15 percent of anorexia nervosa patients die of their illness. Dan Reiff and Kathleen Kim Lampson Reiff report that follow-up studies they reviewed show death rates as high as 18 percent for anorexia and bulimia. And the Canadian National Eating Disorder Information Centre in Toronto warns that both anorexia and bulimia can have severe physical and emotional effects, and in 10 to 20 percent of cases can be fatal.

Eating disorder survivors find the road to recovery difficult. . . . Less than half of patients, about 44 percent, recover well, according to these sources. About 31 percent are intermediate, and 25 percent have poor outcome.

Eating Disorders Take a Heavy Toll

Eating disorders steal time and concentration from other relationships and growing-up activities. They can be associated with alcohol and/or drug abuse, which may increase medical and mental complications. Sufferers lose energy, irritate easily, are lonely and driven to keep their disorder a secret.

Common symptoms include fatigue, lethargy, weakness, impaired concentration, nonfocal abdominal pain, dizziness, faintness, sore muscles, chills, cold sweats, frequent sore throats, diarrhea and constipation, according to Allan Kaplan and Paul Garfinkel in *Medical Issues and the Eating Disorders*.

"I have many regrets. I lost a number of friends, hurt a lot of people I care about," laments one young woman who recovered from anorexia nervosa and bulimia nervosa. "My memories of the last 16 years are spotty and dim. In fact, there have been many major events, such as my sister's wedding, that I have no recollection of. Eighty to 90 percent of my time was spent in (eating) behaviors. My behaviors overtook my life and I essentially lost 16 years of living—years that I can't have back."

The father of a child with an eating disorder said, "She has withdrawn into her own world. She's lonely and is missing out on all the fun and exciting things during her teenage years . . . I have cried many times over this."

Families of eating disordered youth are in a difficult situation. They see their child behaving in destructive ways and feel helpless and frustrated. They may try to gain control over what and how much the teenager chooses to eat. Some police washrooms and search through drawers for diet pills or laxatives. Moms and dads struggle both with the child's problem eating and their own concerns over injury to growth and development. The eating disorder may take over and dominate family life.

The Prevalence of Eating Disorders

Many specialists in the field are convinced that the current high rates of eating disorders in the U.S. are the inevitable result of 60 to 80 million adults dieting, losing weight, rebounding, and learning to be chronic dieters. The majority of chronic dieters are women.

Prevalence has been difficult to determine because of the extremes sufferers take to hide their disorder, limitations of assessments, and public health apathy in compiling national statistics. Current figures are probably under reported. I feel sure we would have more accurate statistics by now if eating disorders had not been kept off the nation's Healthy People 2000 agenda, in what I regard as an effort to protect vested interests in the weight loss industry.

About one in 10 teenagers and college students suffer from eating disorders, 90 to 95 percent of them female, according to the National Eating Disorders Organization. In 1996, Michael Levine compiled figures for the February Eating Disorder Awareness Week giving a "conservative estimate" that 5 to 10 percent of post puberty females are affected by eating disorders which cause significant misery and disruption in their lives. The Canadian Centre reports somewhat higher figures: in addition to those North American women who have anorexia and bulimia, another 10 to 20 percent engage in some of the symptoms on an occasional basis.

These are not solid statistics based on national figures, but rather smaller studies, and many experts suggest the figures are actually much higher.

Evidence of an Increase

Although not conclusive, there is much evidence that eating disorders have increased over the past 30 years, according to Harold Goldstein of the National Institute of Mental Health. The Institute suggests that cases of anorexia and bulimia have doubled over the past decade. Sharp increases have been found among females age 15 to 24, and a study in Scotland found the incidence of anorexia increased over six times between 1965 and 1991.

Most of the eating disorder specialists I network with and many writers in the field are saying that the prevalence has increased in the past decade, eating disorders are striking at younger and younger ages, and they are affecting many more boys and young men.

Nancy King, MS, RD, co-author of *Moving Away from Diets* and a registered dietitian who works with disordered eating in southern California, says she now sees 7- and 8-year-old children with nearly full-blown eating disorders. "Many pediatricians are not recognizing it's an eating problem when a child this young loses 12 pounds over the summer. They're not yet in puberty!"

About 9,000 people are hospitalized annually in the U.S. for the treatment of eating disorders, according to Robin Sesan, PhD, director of the Brandywine Psychotherapy Center in Wilmington, Del.

Widely regarded as a modern problem, eating disorders have been known for centuries. Earlier it was thought eating disorders are most prevalent in middle and upper socioeconomic levels, but there is increasing recognition that they affect people of all income levels, genders and ethnic groups.

Food, Weight, and Relationships

Eating disorders usually consist of two sets of disturbances: first, the problems related to food and weight, and second, problems concerning relationships with oneself and others. They are extremely complex, arising out of both emotional problems and eating disturbances, within a culture that puts great emphasis on thinness and appearance. Some problems may be rooted in families that are overly controlling or disengaged, or who have problems they are unable to acknowledge or deal with openly. Puberty is a critical time.

Often sexual abuse or trauma will be an initiating event. Some specialists see eating disorders as survival strategies developed in response to harassment, racism, homophobia, abuse of power, poverty, or emotional, physical or sexual abuse.

Dieting Disorders

The term "eating disorder" is somewhat misleading because it implies the problem is learning to eat normally again. Given the complex behavioral and psychological components of eating disorders, it isn't that simple.

"Eating disorders should be called dieting disorders, because it is the dieting process and not eating that causes the initiation of both anorexia nervosa and bulimia nervosa," says Joe McVoy, PhD, an eating disorder specialist in Radford, Va.

McVoy says the term "eating disorder" seems to indicate something is wrong with the eating process, whereas what happens is a conscious choice to restrict one's food intake or diet, which leads to starvation and ultimately the disorder.

"Onset of an eating disorder typically follows a period of restrictive dieting; however, only a minority of people who diet develop eating disorders," says the American Dietetic Association in its position paper on eating disorders. . . .

Anorexia Nervosa

"When I first started to eat strangely, all I would eat were sweets, and that wasn't any good. Then I got into just eating salads, just lettuce and diet pop, and that wasn't any good. Then I got into pretty much not eating at all, and that wasn't any good," said a former anorexic patient quoted by Reiff and Lampson Reiff in *Eating Disorders*.

In Levine's statistics, anorexia nervosa affects about one to four of every 400 girls. The Canadian Centre estimates it affects 1 to 3 percent of women in the population.

Anorexia has had some high-profile victims. Singer Karen Carpenter. Gymnast Christy Heinrich.

Actress Tracey Gold, of the ABC sitcom *Growing Pains*, was only 12 when her pediatrician first diagnosed her anorexia. Four months of psychotherapy seemed to get the problem under control and she gained weight, up to 133 pounds by the time she turned 19 in 1988. It was too much, she thought. To lose weight her endocrinologist put her on a 500-calorie-a-day diet and in two months she had dropped to her goal of 113. But during the next three years her weight kept dropping, until in January 1992 at 80 pounds she was hospitalized and had to fight to save her life. . . .

Female athletes and dancers are at high risk for anorexia nervosa. As many as 13 to 22 percent of young women in selected groups of elite runners and dancers have the disorder. Two studies of female dancers cited by Jacqueline Berning and Suzanne Steen, authors of *Sports Nutrition for the 90's*, found between 5 and 22 percent had anorexia nervosa, with a higher incidence among young women competing in national versus regional performances.

Signs and Symptoms

In anorexia nervosa, by definition, the individual is more than 15 percent under expected weight, fears gaining weight, is preoccupied with food, has abnormal eating habits, and has amenorrhea, or if male, a decrease in sexual drive or interest. There are two types: one simply restricts food; the other restricts food and either purges regularly, or binges and purges both, according to the APA *Diagnostic and Statistical Manual.*

Changes occur in behavior, perception, thinking, mood and social interaction. A sense of heightened control and control over food seems important to the person with anorexia. Pleasure and enjoyment during eating are replaced by guilt, anxiety and ambivalence. Mood tends to be depressed, irritable, anxious and unstable, often leading to increased social isolation. Compulsive exercise may be a part of the disorder.

Symptoms are usually evident: emaciated appearance, dry skin, sometimes yellowish, fine body hair, brittle hair and nails, body temperature below 96.6, pulse rate usually below 60 beats per minute, subnormal blood pressure, and sometimes edema, say Kaplan and Garfinkel.

Initially, these are similar to symptoms associated with a restrictive diet: light-headedness, apathy, irritability, and decrease in energy. Then the consequences of prolonged semi-starvation begin to set in and effects worsen. Duration of the disorder may range from a single episode to a lifelong illness. . . .

Bulimia Nervosa

"I can't stop throwing up. I try, I really do. Yesterday, I promised myself I wouldn't do it anymore. I tried to keep myself busy. I cleaned house, played with the cat, prayed. . . . But I don't want to gain weight. I can't do that! I never want to be fat again. I'll never go back there. Nothing is worse than that pain. . . . My joints even hurt. I feel so old. My hair looks horrible; and it keeps falling out. I find it all over the place. My mouth is so full of sores, it's gross! I can't even walk around the house standing straight any more. I'm in a daze. I can't focus. But I can't stop. I feel so trapped. Please help me . . ." said a patient from Lemon Grove, Calif., as quoted in *The Healthy Weigh.*

Bulimia nervosa affects 1 to 3 percent of middle and high school girls, 1 to 4 percent of college women, and 1 to 2 percent among community samples, according to figures compiled by Michael Levine. A recent study of college freshmen found 4.5 percent of females and 0.4 percent of males had a history of bulimia nervosa, say the Reiffs. The National Eating Disorder Information Centre in Canada reports 3 to 5 percent of women in North America have bulimia.

By definition, a person with bulimia nervosa goes on an eating binge at least twice a week, eating a very large amount of food within a discrete period and then tries to compensate either by purging or nonpurging behavior. As the disorder progresses it develops into a complex lifestyle that is increasingly isolating, with depressed mood and low self-esteem.

Self-Abusive Purging Behavior

Vomiting is the most common form of purging, which includes taking laxatives and diuretics. Some bulimics binge and purge many times a day. Patients with bulimia may be of normal weight and seem physically healthy—except for the tell-tale signs of vomiting behavior: finger calluses or lesions on the dominant hand from stimulating the gag reflex (especially in early stages when stimulation is needed to induce vomiting), "chipmunk" cheeks from stimulation of the salivary glands, erosion of enamel (especially on the surface of the upper teeth next to the tongue).

The consequences of self-abusive purging behavior become increasingly obvious as the frequency and duration increase, and include hair loss, fatigue, insomnia, muscle weakness, edema, dizziness, sore throat, stomach pain or cramping, bloating, bad breath and bloodshot eyes. Cardiac arrhythmias affect 20 percent and require emergency treatment. Ipecac syrup abuse may lead to death through cardiomyopathy, myocarditis.

Up to one-third of anorexic individuals develop bulimia nervosa. Bulimia was only recognized in 1980 and listed by the American Psychiatric Association in its *Diagnostic and Statistical Manual*. In 1987 this was replaced by the term bulimia nervosa. It is unclear whether the disorder has been a hidden syndrome, or is relatively new.

Bizarre Behaviors

Many of the physical and mental abnormalities of eating disorders are known to chronic dieters and people who severely restrict their food intake.

The bizarre eating behaviors common to anorexia nervosa are also typical of those described under other starvation conditions. In Ancel Keys' well-known Minnesota Starvation study of the effects of famine in male volunteers who reduced their food intake by 50 percent and lost 25 percent of their weight, the men exhibited many similar behaviors.

As they lost weight, their food interest intensified. The men talked food, fantasized about food, collected recipes, studied cookbooks and menus, and developed odd eating rituals. They would dawdle up to two hours over a meal, toying with their food, cutting it in small pieces, adding spices, sometimes in distasteful ways, trying to make it seem like more and of more variety. They were possessive about food, hoarded food, and spent much time planning, preparing and eating food saved from meals. They ate their allotted food to the last crumb, and some licked their plates. They grew angry when they saw others wasting food.

Feelings related to this kind of behavior are explained by a woman who had recovered from anorexia nervosa and bulimia nervosa, in *Eating Disorders.*

"While anorexic, my body not only anticipated eating, it reveled in it. Being starved and hungry makes the experience of eating more intense—almost sensual. The feeling is analogous to what is experienced when drinking water when extremely thirsty, sleeping after being totally exhausted, or urinating after one's bladder has become overly full. What is usually somewhat ordinary becomes exciting— something to look forward to in an otherwise painful and lonely world. This made changing behaviors so that I no longer experienced intense hunger extremely difficult.". . .

Binge Eating Disorders

Some eating disorders don't fit neatly into these diagnostic criteria. They may have many features of anorexia or bulimia, but involve different eating behaviors, such as repeatedly chewing and spitting out, but not swallowing, large amounts of food.

Levine calls these *atypical eating disorders,* and finds prevalence rates of 2 to 13 percent of middle and high school girls, and 3 to 6 percent of post puberty females in the community.

Binge eating disorder is included in this group. This newly-identified disorder meets the criteria for bulimia nervosa except that individuals do not regularly engage in purging behavior and do not meet the criteria for being unduly concerned with weight and shape. They eat large amounts of food at least twice a week, in a relatively short time, with a sense of loss of control. They may be of average weight, but most often are overweight.

This disorder was first described in 1959, and is similar to what has been called "compulsive eating." Research on binge eating is still in its infancy.

Excessive Exercise

One of the fastest growing eating disorder behaviors since 1992 is excessive exercise or exercise addiction to lose weight or sculpt the body, says McVoy. Many anorectic and bulimic patients deal with some form of exercise dependency, explains Karin Kratina, MA, RD, an exercise physiologist and registered dietitian at the Renfrew Center in Florida.

Excessive exercise aimed at weight loss is regarded as a secondary dependency, usually to an eating disorder, says Kratina. Physical activity takes priority over everything else for the exercise-dependent individual. He or she follows stereotyped patterns, continues exercising even when it causes or aggravates a serious physical disorder. There may be severe withdrawal symptoms upon stopping exercise.

"Stress injuries are common, and frequently the person exercises right through an injury so it can't heal properly," reports Kratina.

Anorexia and bodybuilding have many similarities, points out David Schlundt, PhD, an eating disorder specialist at Vanderbilt University in Nashville. "There are special diets, use of diuretics, steroid use, obsessive exercise, very low fat diets, and so on. An obsession with changing size and shape of the body leads to extreme and sometimes dangerous changes in diet, exercise and substance abuse."

One of the reasons eating disorders are increasing among young men is likely a result of this new obsession with muscles and body sculpting. Boys are reflecting a dissatisfaction with their natural bodies and an intense desire to alter their appearance, McVoy says. . . .

The Link to Sexual and Physical Abuse

Sexual abuse is a common experience of many eating disorder patients, says Susan Wooley, PhD, professor of psychology and co-director of the Eating Disorders Clinic at the University of Cincinnati Medical College.

Until very recently, the importance of a history of sexual or physical abuse was minimized by the mostly male therapists who dominated the field in research, publishing and conferences. Wooley calls it the "concealed debate" which women therapists held in conference hallways, and is finally being recognized.

The National Women's Study, a national random sample of 4,008 adult women in the U.S. who were interviewed at least three times over the course of one year, found that women with bulimia nervosa were twice as likely to have been raped (27 percent vs 13 percent) or sexually molested (22 vs 12 percent), and four times as likely to have experienced aggravated assault (27 vs 8 percent) as women without an eating disorder.

Over half the women with bulimia reported a lifetime history of some type of criminal victimization event, compared to less than one-third of women who did not have an eating disorder (54 vs 31 percent).

Twelve percent of women with bulimia nervosa had been raped as children, at age 11 or younger, compared with 5 percent of women without an eating disorder. The age at the time of rape predated the age of the first binge episode in all cases, suggesting childhood sexual abuse as a causal factor.

Even so, the true extent of sexual abuse is unknown due to silencing of the victims and their reluctance to disclose abuse even to therapists trained to help them in this area. . . .

Wooley reports that the predominantly female patients more often disclose histories of sexual abuse to female therapists. Male therapists as a whole did not realize the extent and consequences of sexual abuse until recently. . . .

Eating disorder specialists Mark Schwartz and Leigh Cohn point out that the rate of sexual abuse was estimated at only 1 in 1,000 in a major psychiatric textbook of the 1960s. But by the 1980s many publications were reporting sexual abuse of one in three females and one in seven males. . . .

This abuse information is all so new that there is wide variation in reports. Further investigation is needed to clarify the issues. What should be considered sexual abuse? How can it be assessed in a reliable way? How can experts cope with the difficulty of disclosure?

At the same time it needs to be recognized that many eating-disordered clients were not sexually or physically abused, and many sexually abused youngsters do not develop eating disorders.

Roots of Eating Disorders

Factors that increase a dieter's vulnerability to eating disorders are believed to be genetic, biological, psychological, sociocultural and familial, as well as a history of sexual or physical abuse.

The traditional patriarchal view holds that the roots of eating disorders lie with pathological traits of patients and their families.

But society has to take responsibility for the tremendous impact of idealizing an increasingly thin female body.

In less than two decades, the acceptable female body size has been whittled down by one-third, writes Patricia Fallon, Melanie Katzman and Wooley, editors of *Feminist Perspectives on Eating Disorders*. Most women no longer fit that size, and trying to do so takes up more and more of their lives. Some are pushed to an apparent point of no return by "our era's culminating demand that women give up nourishment and a large share of their bodies."

For some girls entering adolescence, accepting their rapidly-changing bodies becomes nearly impossible when placed against this cultural backdrop. Not only are their female role models extremely thin and usually dieting, but males they know are often openly denigrating large women and admiring thin women.

THE ABCS OF EATING DISORDERS

Lee Hoffman

Lee Hoffman, a staff member of the Office of Scientific Information (OSI), National Institute of Mental Health (NIMH), describes the typical symptoms and possible causes of eating disorders. These disorders, the author explains, are not unique to young females: Males and females, young and old, of all racial and ethnic groups can develop them. Hoffman stresses that treatment can save the life of a friend or family member who has an eating disorder. The more people know about eating disorders, explains Hoffman, the better equipped they are to encourage treatment and to provide support and understanding for a friend or family member struggling with one.

Each year millions of people in the United States develop serious and sometimes life-threatening eating disorders. The vast majority—more than 90 percent—of those afflicted with eating disorders are adolescent and young adult women. One reason that women in this age group are particularly vulnerable to eating disorders is their tendency to go on strict diets to achieve an "ideal" figure. Researchers have found that such stringent dieting can play a key role in triggering eating disorders.

Approximately 1 percent of adolescent girls develop anorexia nervosa, a dangerous condition in which they can literally starve themselves to death. Another 2 to 3 percent of young women develop bulimia nervosa, a destructive pattern of excessive overeating followed by vomiting or other "purging" behaviors to control their weight. These eating disorders also occur in men and older women, but much less frequently. The consequences of eating disorders can be severe, with 1 in 10 cases of anorexia nervosa leading to death from starvation, cardiac arrest, or suicide. Fortunately, increasing awareness of the dangers of eating disorders—sparked by medical studies and extensive media coverage of the illness—has led many people to seek help. Nevertheless, some people with eating disorders refuse to admit that they have a problem and do not get treatment. Family members and friends can help recognize the problem and encourage the person to seek treatment. . . .

Excerpted from Lee Hoffman, *Eating Disorders*, U.S. Dept. of Health and Human Services, National Institute of Mental Health, NIH Publication no. 93-3477, January 1993.

Anorexia Nervosa

People who intentionally starve themselves suffer from an eating disorder called anorexia nervosa. The disorder, which usually begins in young people around the time of puberty, involves extreme weight loss—at least 15 percent below the individual's normal body weight. Many people with the disorder look emaciated but are convinced they are overweight. Sometimes they must be hospitalized to prevent starvation.

> Deborah developed anorexia nervosa when she was 16. A rather shy, studious teenager, she tried hard to please everyone. She had an attractive appearance, but was slightly overweight. Like many teenage girls, she was interested in boys but concerned that she wasn't pretty enough to get their attention. When her father jokingly remarked that she would never get a date if she didn't take off some weight, she took him seriously and began to diet relentlessly—never believing she was thin enough even when she became extremely underweight.
>
> Soon after the pounds started dropping off, Deborah's menstrual periods stopped. As anorexia tightened its grip, she became obsessed with dieting and food and developed strange eating rituals. Every day she weighed all the food she would eat on a kitchen scale, cutting solids into minuscule pieces and precisely measuring liquids. She would then put her daily ration in small containers, lining them up in neat rows. She also exercised compulsively, even after she weakened and became faint. She never took an elevator if she could walk up steps.
>
> No one was able to convince Deborah that she was in danger. Finally, her doctor insisted that she be hospitalized and carefully monitored for treatment of her illness. While in the hospital, she secretly continued her exercise regimen in the bathroom, doing strenuous routines of situps and knee-bends. It took several hospitalizations and a good deal of individual and family outpatient therapy for Deborah to face and solve her problems.

Deborah's case is not unusual. People with anorexia typically starve themselves, even though they suffer terribly from hunger pains. One of the most frightening aspects of the disorder is that people with anorexia continue to think they are overweight even when they are bone-thin. For reasons not yet understood, they become terrified of gaining any weight.

Food and weight become obsessions. For some, the compulsiveness shows up in strange eating rituals or the refusal to eat in front of others. It is not uncommon for people with anorexia to collect recipes and prepare gourmet feasts for family and friends, but not partake in the meals themselves. Like Deborah, they may adhere to strict exercise routines to keep off weight. Loss of monthly menstrual periods is typical in women with the disorder. Men with anorexia often become impotent.

Bulimia Nervosa

People with bulimia nervosa consume large amounts of food and then rid their bodies of the excess calories by vomiting, abusing laxatives or diuretics, taking enemas, or exercising obsessively. Some use a combination of all these forms of purging. Because many individuals with bulimia "binge and purge" in secret and maintain normal or above normal body weight, they can often successfully hide their problem from others for years.

> Lisa developed bulimia nervosa at 18. Like Deborah, her strange eating behavior began when she started to diet. She too dieted and exercised to lose weight, but unlike Deborah, she regularly ate huge amounts of food and maintained her normal weight by forcing herself to vomit. Lisa often felt like an emotional powder keg—angry, frightened, and depressed.
>
> Unable to understand her own behavior, she thought no one else would either. She felt isolated and lonely. Typically, when things were not going well, she would be overcome with an uncontrollable desire for sweets. She would eat pounds of candy and cake at a time, and often not stop until she was exhausted or in severe pain. Then, overwhelmed with guilt and disgust, she would make herself vomit.
>
> Her eating habits so embarrassed her that she kept them secret until, depressed by her mounting problems, she attempted suicide. Fortunately, she didn't succeed. While recuperating in the hospital, she was referred to an eating disorders clinic where she became involved in group therapy. There she received medications to treat the illness and the understanding and help she so desperately needed from others who had the same problem.

Family, friends, and physicians may have difficulty detecting bulimia in someone they know. Many individuals with the disorder remain at normal body weight or above because of their frequent binges and purges, which can range from once or twice a week to several times a day. Dieting heavily between episodes of binging and purging is also common. Eventually, half of those with anorexia will develop bulimia.

As with anorexia, bulimia typically begins during adolescence. The condition occurs most often in women but is also found in men. Many individuals with bulimia, ashamed of their strange habits, do not seek help until they reach their thirties or forties. By this time, their eating behavior is deeply ingrained and more difficult to change.

Binge Eating Disorder

An illness that resembles bulimia nervosa is binge eating disorder. Like bulimia, the disorder is characterized by episodes of uncontrolled eating or binging. However, binge eating disorder differs from bulimia because its sufferers do not purge their bodies of excess food.

Individuals with binge eating disorder feel that they lose control of themselves when eating. They eat large quantities of food and do not stop until they are uncomfortably full. Usually, they have more difficulty losing weight and keeping it off than do people with other serious weight problems. Most people with the disorder are obese and have a history of weight fluctuations. Binge eating disorder is found in about 2 percent of the general population—more often in women than men. Recent research shows that binge eating disorder occurs in about 30 percent of people participating in medically supervised weight control programs. . . .

Causes of Eating Disorders

In trying to understand the causes of eating disorders, scientists have studied the personalities, genetics, environments, and biochemistry of people with these illnesses. As is often the case, the more that is learned, the more complex the roots of eating disorders appear.

Most people with eating disorders share certain personality traits: low self-esteem, feelings of helplessness, and a fear of becoming fat. In anorexia, bulimia, and binge eating disorder, eating behaviors seem to develop as a way of handling stress and anxieties.

People with anorexia tend to be "too good to be true." They rarely disobey, keep their feelings to themselves, and tend to be perfectionists, good students, and excellent athletes. Some researchers believe that people with anorexia restrict food—particularly carbohydrates—to gain a sense of control in some area of their lives. Having followed the wishes of others for the most part, they have not learned how to cope with the problems typical of adolescence, growing up, and becoming independent. Controlling their weight appears to offer two advantages, at least initially: they can take control of their bodies and gain approval from others. However, it eventually becomes clear to others that they are out-of-control and dangerously thin.

People who develop bulimia and binge eating disorder typically consume huge amounts of food—often junk food—to reduce stress and relieve anxiety. With binge eating, however, comes guilt and depression. Purging can bring relief, but it is only temporary. Individ-

uals with bulimia are also impulsive and more likely to engage in risky behavior such as abuse of alcohol and drugs.

Genetic and Environmental Factors

Eating disorders appear to run in families—with female relatives most often affected. This finding suggests that genetic factors may predispose some people to eating disorders; however, other influences—both behavioral and environmental—may also play a role. One recent study found that mothers who are overly concerned about their daughters' weight and physical attractiveness may put the girls at increased risk of developing an eating disorder. In addition, girls with eating disorders often have fathers and brothers who are overly critical of their weight.

Although most victims of anorexia and bulimia are adolescent and young adult women, these illnesses can also strike men and older women. Anorexia and bulimia are found most often in Caucasians, but these illnesses also affect African Americans and other racial ethnic groups. People pursuing professions or activities that emphasize thinness—like modeling, dancing, gymnastics, wrestling, and long-distance running—are more susceptible to the problem. In contrast to other eating disorders, one-third to one-fourth of all patients with binge eating disorder are men. Preliminary studies also show that the condition occurs equally among African Americans and Caucasians.

The Neuroendocrine System

In an attempt to understand eating disorders, scientists have studied the biochemical functions of people with the illnesses. They have focused recently on the neuroendocrine system—a combination of the central nervous and hormonal systems. Through complex but carefully balanced feedback mechanisms, the neuroendocrine system regulates sexual function, physical growth and development, appetite and digestion, sleep, heart and kidney function, emotions, thinking, and memory—in other words, multiple functions of the mind and body. Many of these regulatory mechanisms are seriously disturbed in people with eating disorders.

In the central nervous system—particularly the brain—key chemical messengers known as neurotransmitters control hormone production. Scientists have found that the neurotransmitters serotonin and norepinephrine function abnormally in people affected by depression. Recently, researchers funded by the National Institute of Mental Health (NIMH) have learned that these neurotransmitters are also decreased in acutely ill anorexia and bulimia patients and long-term recovered anorexia patients. Because many people with eating disorders also appear to suffer from depression, some scientists believe that there may be a link between these two disorders. This link is supported by studies showing that antidepressants can be used successfully to treat some people with eating disorders. In fact, new research has suggested that some patients with anorexia may respond well to the antidepressant medication fluoxetine, which affects serotonin function in the body.

People with either anorexia or certain forms of depression also tend to have higher than normal levels of cortisol, a brain hormone released in response to stress. Scientists have been able to show that the excess levels of cortisol in both anorexia and depression are caused by a problem that occurs in or near a region of the brain called the hypothalamus.

In addition to connections between depression and eating disorders, scientists have found biochemical similarities between people with eating disorders and obsessive-compulsive disorder (OCD). Just as serotonin levels are known to be abnormal in people with depression and eating disorders, they are also abnormal in patients with OCD. Recently, NIMH researchers have found that many patients with bulimia have obsessive-compulsive behavior as severe as that seen in patients actually diagnosed with OCD. Conversely, patients with OCD frequently have abnormal eating behaviors.

The hormone vasopressin is another brain chemical found to be abnormal in people with eating disorders and OCD. NIMH researchers have shown that levels of this hormone are elevated in patients with OCD, anorexia, and bulimia. Normally released in response to physical and possibly emotional stress, vasopressin may contribute to the obsessive behavior seen in some patients with eating disorders.

NIMH-supported investigators are also exploring the role of other brain chemicals in eating behavior. Many are conducting studies in animals to shed some light on human disorders. For example, scientists have found that levels of neuropeptide Y and peptide YY, recently shown to be elevated in patients with anorexia and bulimia, stimulate eating behavior in laboratory animals. Other investigators have found that cholecystokinin (CCK), a hormone known to be low in some women with bulimia, causes laboratory animals to feel full and stop eating. This finding may possibly explain why women with bulimia do not feel satisfied after eating and continue to binge. . . .

Treatment

It cannot be overemphasized how important treatment is—the sooner, the better. The longer abnormal eating behaviors persist, the more difficult it is to overcome the disorder and its effects on the body. In some cases, long-term treatment may be requested. Families and friends offering support and encouragement can play an important role in the success of the treatment program. . . .

The complex interaction of emotional and physiological problems in eating disorders calls for a comprehensive treatment plan, involving a variety of experts and approaches. Ideally, the treatment team includes an internist, a nutritionist, an individual psychotherapist, a group and family psychotherapist, and a psychopharmacologist—someone who is knowledgeable about psychoactive medications useful in treating these disorders.

To help those with eating disorders deal with their illness and underlying emotional issues, some form of psychotherapy is usually needed. A psychiatrist, psychologist, or other mental health professional meets with the patient individually and provides ongoing emotional support, while the patient begins to understand and cope with the illness. Group therapy, in which people share their experiences with others who have similar problems, has been especially effective for individuals with bulimia.

Use of individual psychotherapy, family therapy, and cognitive-behavioral therapy—a form of psychotherapy that teaches patients how to change abnormal thoughts and behavior—is often the most productive. Cognitive-behavior therapists focus on changing eating behaviors usually by rewarding or modeling wanted behavior. These therapists also help patients work to change the distorted and rigid thinking patterns associated with eating disorders.

NIMH-supported scientists have examined the effectiveness of combining psychotherapy and medications. In a recent study of bulimia, researchers found that both intensive group therapy and antidepressant medications, combined or alone, benefited patients. In another study of bulimia, the combined use of cognitive-behavioral therapy and antidepressant medications was most beneficial. The combination treatment was particularly effective in preventing relapse once medications were discontinued. For patients with binge eating disorder, cognitive-behavioral therapy and antidepressant medications may also prove to be useful. . . .

The efforts of mental health professionals need to be combined with those of other health professionals to obtain the best treatment. Physicians treat any medical complications, and nutritionists advise on diet and eating regimens. . . .

Helping the Person with an Eating Disorder

Treatment can save the life of someone with an eating disorder. Friends, relatives, teachers, and physicians all play an important role in helping the ill person start and stay with a treatment program. Encouragement, caring, and persistence, as well as information about eating disorders and their dangers, may be needed to convince the ill person to get help, stick with treatment, or try again.

Family members and friends can call local hospitals or university medical centers to find out about eating disorder clinics and clinicians experienced in treating the illnesses. For college students, treatment programs may be available in school counseling centers.

Family members and friends should read as much as possible about eating disorders so they can help the person with the illness understand his or her problem. Many local mental health organizations and self-help groups provide free literature on eating disorders. Some of these groups also provide treatment program referrals and information on local self-help groups. Once the person gets help, he or she will continue to need lots of understanding and encouragement to stay in treatment.

NIMH continues its search for new and better treatments for eating disorders. . . . This research promises to yield even more hope for patients and their families by providing a greater understanding of the causes and complexities of eating disorders.

NOT JUST A YOUNG WOMAN'S PROBLEM

Joel M. Roselin

According to writer Joel M. Roselin, thousands of women in their forties, fifties, and sixties who suffered from anorexia, bulimia, or binge eating when they were teenagers or young adults continue to struggle with these disorders. For many women, he explains, the stresses of midlife—such as menopause, conflicts about sex, and social pressure to stay young and thin—trigger the onset or reoccurrence of an eating disorder. Although older women tend not to seek treatment for their eating disorders, Roselin points out, it is important for them to get treatment because they are more susceptible to such serious health risks as osteoporosis.

Carol Stephens (name has been changed) was having trouble sleeping. At 1 a.m., she put her coat and shoes on over her pajamas and walked to the nearest convenience store. There, she bought a large box of cookies. She lay in bed in the dark and didn't stop eating them until she'd finished every crumb.

Carol was showing symptoms of an eating disorder—something we usually associate with teenagers and women in their 20s. Carol, however, is no teenager. She is a 43-year-old woman.

She is far from alone. "While most women with eating disorders develop the problem before age 20, only 50% report being cured." "What this means," says Vivian Hanson Meehan, president of ANAD—National Association of Anorexia Nervosa and Associated Disorders, "is that thousands of midlife women continue to suffer." Some have anorexia nervosa: an unwillingness or inability to eat enough to maintain normal weight, along with an exaggerated fear of gaining weight. Others have bulimia, a disease in which women binge on large amounts of food and then vomit or use laxatives, diuretics, diet pills, strict dieting or excessive exercise to prevent weight gain. Another common eating disorder among midlife women is binge eating. Like Carol, binge eaters devour large amounts of food at one time but do not "purge" afterward by throwing up.

From Joel M. Roselin, "Eating Disorders: Not Just a Young Woman's Problem." This article was originally published in *Seasons®* magazine, volume 7, issue 5, and is reprinted with permission.

Midlife Triggers

Although a small number of women with eating disorders develop them for the first time in midlife, most have a history of such problems dating back to their teens or twenties. Whether symptoms are a relapse or the first onset of an eating disorder, experts agree that midlife stresses can be a trigger.

Like puberty, menopause changes a woman's image of herself as a sexual being. "At 13 the question is, what does it mean to have a period?" explains David Herzog, M.D., director of the Eating Disorder Unit at Massachusetts General Hospital and associate professor of psychiatry at Harvard Medical School. "And at menopause, what does it mean *not* to?"

Adolescents sometimes stop eating in the hope that they won't develop a womanly shape, which they perceive as ugly and fat. In fact, many girls with anorexia *do* stop developing breasts and menstruating. Mature women with eating disorders may be expressing similar anxieties that they've managed to suppress for years. They, too, may express conflicts about sex by either overeating or under-eating.

Another contributor to eating disorders in midlife is the social pressure to stay young. There is a natural tendency for both men and women to gain weight as they age—in part because metabolism slows. But in our society, weight gain and aging in women are considered taboo. This makes it more difficult to accept the aging process. "What used to be considered an acceptable shape is no longer acceptable," says Dr. Herzog. "And some women are single at midlife, which can make them more self-conscious about their looks."

Faced with such intense midlife pressures, some women react by binge eating. "I know when the problem started for me," says Jan Simon, a 62-year-old mother of two grown children. "After my husband was hospitalized with hepatitis, I headed straight for the Chinese buffet. Stuffing myself was a comfort, but after each binge I would feel awful. And the worse I felt about myself, the more I binged."

There is a complex relationship between negative emotions and eating disorders. "If a woman starts a diet when she feels troubled, she is more likely to develop an eating disorder—especially if she had one in the past," says George Hsu, M.D., director of the Eating Disorders Program at New England Medical Center in Boston.

In turn, poor eating habits can affect mood and energy. "Many people don't realize how nutrition affects their feelings and behavior," points out Barbara Lynne, L.I. C.S.W., a psychotherapist who runs an over-35 eating disorder support group in Newton, Massachusetts. "Vitamin and mineral deficiencies, which often accompany eating disorders, can make you feel fatigued and depressed."

Increased Health Risks

Older women are less likely than younger ones to get treatment for eating disorders, says Ruth Striegel-Moore, Ph.D., professor of psychology at Wesleyan University in Middletown, Connecticut. "Seeking therapy was less acceptable a generation ago," she points out. "And unlike teenage girls, grown women aren't being closely watched by their parents." But getting help is more important than ever in midlife because the health risks associated with eating disorders can be serious. For example, underweight women often have reduced bone mass. This can contribute to osteoporosis and an increased risk of fracture. Women who vomit repeatedly may develop ulcers, esophageal tears, dehydration, dental and gum disease and kidney problems. At the other end of the spectrum, extreme binge eating can cause the stomach to perforate. And all women with eating disorders are at risk for developing vitamin and mineral deficiencies which, in turn, can cause a variety of ailments.

Doctors treat binge eaters with a supervised weight-loss program. For women who have anorexia or more rarely bulimia, they may prescribe liquid nutritional supplements. Patients with alarmingly low body weights are usually hospitalized and fed through a tube until they are out of danger. Serious eating disorders require proper psychologic or psychiatric care.

Older and Wiser

Once doctors are convinced that a woman is getting proper nutrition, they can begin working on the emotional problems that contribute to her disorder, using a combination of psychotherapy and medication. Gaining insight and changing behavior are at the heart of a recovery program. "Eating disorders may fall into the category of addiction and are extremely difficult to drop. Learning and practicing a healthy lifestyle and discussing feelings with a therapist often helps women let go of addictive behaviors," says Ms. Lynne.

Carol Stephens' busy schedule allowed her little time for self-care. She binged for comfort and to gain an energy burst. With help from Ms. Lynne, Carol now uses that time to read, take a walk or call friends in her support group.

In therapy, Ms. Lynne helped Carol become more mindful when eating. "She encouraged me to taste and feel the food," Carol says. One day I got halfway through an ice cream sundae and realized I didn't really want it. So I just threw it away!"

Another technique that worked for Carol was allowing herself to binge for 5 minutes. When the time was up, she wrote down how she felt before, during and after eating. "This made me more aware of my feelings and behavior, and how the two were connected," she says.

After a year, Carol learned how to maintain her weight without yo-

yo dieting. Now, she is beginning to lose weight slowly but effectively. "When I'm tempted to binge, I ask, 'Is this stomach hunger or emotional hunger?' I've learned to feed emotional hunger by turning to friends or family members and my support group."

"When I was lonely and wanting love, food was always there for me," she says. "But I could never get enough. Now, finally, my desire to be healthy outweighs my desire to overeat."

DIETING: A TRIGGER FOR EATING DISORDERS

Beatrice Trum Hunter

In the following selection, writer Beatrice Trum Hunter states that eating disorders have become increasingly common, especially among adolescent girls. Dieting affects the likelihood of developing eating disorders, Hunter warns. At the same time that many young people have become overweight due to lack of exercise and poor food choices, pressure to be thin is on the upswing, she writes, leading teenagers to try to control dietary intake through crash diets. Some of these young people develop unhealthy and unrealistic attitudes about food and become obsessed with dieting, Hunter explains, resulting in an eating disorder.

According to the American Academy of Pediatrics, 30% of American school-age children are overweight. Half of them will grow into overweight adults. . . .

Factors attributed to childhood obesity include poor food choices and sedentary habits. Fast food meals—often favorite choices—typically contain 40% to 50% of their calories from fat, but these foods are low in fiber, iron, and vitamins A and C. As for lack of exercise, the title of an article in a medical publication summarized the problem: "Profusion of TV produces plump couch-potato tots." By adolescence, a child has watched 15,000 hours of television, and has been exposed to 350,000 commercials, more than half of which promote highly processed food products and soft drinks.

Linked to this problem of childhood obesity are various attempts to control dietary intake. At times, well-intentioned pressures may lead to unintended and regrettable developments. Eating disorders may develop during the adolescent years, and parents need to be aware of warning signs and symptoms. There is an emerging preoccupation with "healthy eating" and fitness among some adolescents, especially girls, that may lead to eating disorders, according to Dr. David S. Rosen, director of adolescent health at the Medical Center of the University of Michigan at Ann Arbor. According to Rosen, healthy eating for teenage girls parallels the "vilification of fat in the media

Excerpted from Beatrice Trum Hunter, "Eating Disorders: Perilous Compulsions," *Consumers' Research Magazine*, September 1997, by permission of the publisher.

and the increasing availability and aggressive marketing of low-fat and no-fat food options." Rosen observes that moderately limiting fat intake may be desirable, but when carried to an extreme, "the compulsive avoidance of fat begins to take on the characteristics of an eating disorder and probably requires the same kind of intervention."

Pressure to be thin is increasing. Over the last few decades, Playboy centerfold models and Miss America contestants have become leaner, with smaller busts and hips. By contrast, the average female between 17 and 24 has become heavier and heavier.

Despite the plethora of weight-reducing diets, meals-in-cans, pills, low-fat products, non-caloric sweeteners, gym equipment, exercise programs, sweat boxes, and other approaches, young people, as well as other segments of the population, are becoming more and more obese. According to the Centers for Disease Control and Prevention, Americans are more overweight now than at any time since the government began to keep complete statistics in the 1960s. At present, 14% of children aged six to 11 and 12% of those aged 12 to 17 are dangerously overweight.

Dieting Puts People at Risk

"Dieting is a chief cause of obesity in America," according to Professor Judith Rodin of Yale University. "Some middle-class parents trying to save their daughters from the stigma of fat insist on severe diets, but depriving children of food may only make them more interested in eating. At some early stage in infancy, people, as well as animals, are pretty well biologically regulated. It takes something to deregulate that system. And one of the things that we know that does that is dieting. That kind of girth control begins to slow down the metabolic rate, and makes the body begin to change in order to protect itself against the reduction in calories. This causes more problems when the dieter returns to eating normally."

Weight cycling—popularly called "yo yo" dieting—attracts many young women. Studies have shown that repeated attempts to lose weight followed by weight gains greatly increase the risk for developing heart disease. Also, people who diet frequently may develop a preference for high-fat and sugary foods, resulting in increased weight.

Crash diets, which depend on drastic calorie reduction to induce weight loss, often backfire and result in weight gain. Severely restricted caloric intake triggers a body response that slows the rate at which calories are used for daily activities. The body adjusts itself to run on fewer calories, and it becomes more efficient in using the available calories in order to conserve its nutrient reserves. When weight loss plateaus, many dieters become frustrated and return to their previous eating habits. However, since the body has learned to function with fewer calories, it stores more calories from the regular diet in the form of fat. The initial pounds lost on a crash diet are mostly water, released by the metabolic changes that occurred as the system adapted to reduced calories. However, the pounds regained are stored as fat. The weight gain will continue until the body returns to its former rate of processing nutrients. Thus, many crash dieters may gain back more weight than they lost on the diet.

Dieting is especially common among adolescent girls and young women who typically report weight concerns and who attempt to restrict their fat or caloric intake as early as age nine or ten years. In the last few decades, the prevalence of such concerns and subsequent efforts to diet have risen dramatically. Eating disorders are now the third most common illness among adolescent females. More than one in five girls score in the abnormal range on tests of eating attitudes and behaviors, and abnormal scores are noted commonly in girls as young as fourth and fifth graders.

Although these problems are encountered mainly with females, adolescent boys and young men with severely abnormal eating habits are being identified more frequently as well.

Dieting by teenagers, from infrequent to uninterrupted, is a sign of possible eating disorders. Parents should be alert to this. Rosen says that eating disorders occur on a continuum, ranging from mild to serious manifestations.

The Main Eating Disorders

Anorexia Nervosa. On the continuum of eating disorders, anorexia nervosa is in the extreme of the range. It has long been recognized as a serious health problem, thought to result from emotional or psychological stresses. The typical patient is a white middle- to upper-middle class young woman, but increasingly, cases are reported among some women of other ages, in males, and in non-whites.

Typically, an anorexic refuses to maintain weight that is above the lowest weight considered to be normal for her age and height. Her total body weight is at least 15% below normal. She displays an intense fear of weight gain, despite the fact that she may be severely underweight. Regarding herself in a mirror, she has a distorted image of her body and is convinced that she is fat. Frequently, she fails to menstruate. She suffers a pathological loss of appetite, accompanied by nutritional deficiency symptoms. . . .

Bulimia Nervosa. Bulimia nervosa is another serious eating disorder of young people, characterized by repeated binge eating and purging. The episodes may be repeated frequently. The person—usually a young woman—consumes excessive amounts of food within a brief period of time, and then induces vomiting or uses a laxative, diuretic, or enema to get rid of the food. When not binging, the bulimic may adhere to a strict dieting or fasting regime, or indulge in vigorous exercise, in attempting to prevent weight gain. . . .

Recent studies by Christopher G. Fairburn and his associates at Oxford University have pinpointed some of the psychological risk factors in early childhood that can contribute to bulimia at a later stage. Frequently, at an early age, the children had viewed themselves with extreme disdain. They had experienced minimal contacts with their parents, or were physically or sexually abused. They encountered parental conflicts or criticisms. The parents themselves frequently had suffered from obesity or bouts of depression. Many of the parents had demanded perfection. Many of the children who later developed bulimia had wrestled with obesity early in life, or had other health problems. Early menstruation, accompanied by body-shape changes, spurred dieting. Bouts of depression or other mental conditions often preceded bulimia. Current dieting by other family members or their critical comments about dieting reinforced the problem. . . .

Binge Eating. Binge eating, a related eating disorder, has some features similar to bulimia, but is regarded as a distinct entity by medical doctors. Even less is known about binge eating than anorexia or bulimia. It is estimated that about 2% of the general American population is affected. Bingers may comprise about 30% of all individuals who attend weight-control programs in hospital settings. An even larger percentage of bingers may exist among some members of the population, such as obese patients who suffer from compulsive mental disorders. . . .

Eating disorders are complex and cannot be treated solely with dietary means. Individual cases may need to address fundamental psychological, familial, societal, and cultural aspects of the disorder.

CAUSE FOR CONCERN: OVERWEIGHT AND OBESITY

The Economist

Overweight and obesity are on the increase in America, according to the *Economist*, a British news magazine. The authors cite statistics showing that in 1997 more than one-half of all Americans were overweight. They attribute this trend to one of two causes—either Americans are eating more or they are not exercising as much as they used to. The authors point out that Americans continue to gain weight in spite of the many weight-loss programs on the market and the concern expressed by doctors and nutritionists about the health risks associated with overweight and obesity. At the same time, the authors note, attitudes toward these two conditions have become more tolerant.

Recently a mother brought her obese son to the clinic that Carmen Mikhail runs for eating disorders at Texas Children's Hospital. Dr Mikhail asked her what the hefty lad drank. "He drinks Coke," said his mother. "But that's fat-free."

Many Americans seem to be under similar misapprehensions. To the dismay of doctors, their body mass (broadly, their weight relative to their height), which held steady through the 1970s, seems to have risen sharply since 1980. The most recent official figures, from the National Centre for Health Statistics, show that more than half of all Americans are now overweight, and that the proportion, especially of the heaviest, is still rising. Yet, as the proportion of fat Americans rises, so does tolerance of tubbiness.

All told, 54.4% of adult Americans are overweight and 22.5% are obese. Some groups are even plumper. Women are more likely to be obese than men. Middle-aged women are especially prone to spread: 35.6% of those in their fifties are obese. So are black women, 37.4% of whom are obese, compared with 24.9% of all women. High-school drop-outs of both sexes are fatter than those with more education. Non-smokers are chubbier than smokers. But, in every group, the story is the same: since the start of the 1980s, the proportion of the fattest has grown fastest.

Reprinted from "That Other National Expansion," editorial, *The Economist*, December 20, 1997, by permission. Copyright ©1997, The Economist, Ltd. Distributed by New York Times Special Features/Syndication Sales.

For this national expansion there can only be two explanations: Americans are eating more, or exercising less. Oddly, the official figures suggest that Americans are eating less fat than in the early 1980s. But these figures are based on what people say they eat. As Americans forget how to cook, they probably know less about what they are swallowing than they once did. Roughly half a family's food budget now goes on food eaten out; and 45% of dinners eaten at home include not a single home-made item.

Exercise is also becoming a rarity. William Dietz, of the Centres for Disease Prevention and Control, notes that, even at the start of high school, only 30% of girls regularly exercise vigorously, and half of these stop before they leave. One American in four admits to being completely sedentary, and another 40% rarely exercise. This is doleful news: a recent study of people who had both lost weight and stayed slim found that exercise was the key to their success. "It's much harder", says Barbara Moore, head of a lobby called Shape Up America!, "to get people to take physical exercise than to change their eating habits."

Helping Americans to shed weight is big business. The biggest market is for low-calorie food and slimming concoctions. Drug treatments, wildly popular in 1996, are now frowned on by doctors. But enrolments at Weight Watchers are 50% up on 1996 and the company, as always, is looking forward to a bumper January in 1998.

Extra Pounds Affect Health

Does it matter if Americans are fatter? Doctors such as George Blackburn, a Harvard nutritionist, are keen to point to the health risks associated with all these extra pounds. "It costs $60 billion–80 billion a year, or almost 10% of all health spending, to treat health problems associated with obesity," he says.

Unfortunately for the campaigners, although links between obesity and poor health are well established, it has been hard to correlate rising weight and national health. Cholesterol levels and hypertension—two ills that usually go with obesity—have been declining, and the increase in a third, adult diabetes, has been small. However, the explanation may partly be better monitoring and treatment.

A greater disincentive to gorging should be the effect on self-esteem and earnings. A study in the *New England Journal of Medicine* four years ago established that fatties are significantly less likely to get married than their slimmer contemporaries. They are also likelier to have lower incomes in early adult life regardless of their skills or social background, something that may partly be the result of discrimination at work.

Tolerance Grows as Waistlines Spread

But, as the tubbies have become the majority, attitudes have become more tolerant. An annual study of eating trends by the NPD Group, a

New York consultancy, finds that the percentage of homemakers who think that "people who are not overweight look a lot more attractive" has slumped from 55% in 1985 to 28% in 1996. And the National Association to Advance Fat Acceptance, which describes itself as a "human-rights" group, runs a dating service and an on-line bulletin board on which 500-pounders can swap tips on where to buy cycling shorts and whether diets work.

Companies that once ignored the tubby now court them, especially in the clothing business. In all, reports the NPD Group, the dollar value of big-sized women's clothes has been creeping up, from 23.5% of the market in 1994 to 25% in 1995 and 1996. Plump ladies, according to a survey in 1996 by Kurt Salmon Associates, a management consultancy, tend to buy in speciality shops, which account for 29% of sales of larger garments, a bigger share than for other sizes. A growing number of companies now offer special labels for the heavyweight. Brylane, one of the market leaders, sells clothes up to size 60, and finds that a third of its large-size business is in 28 (ie, a 45-inch waist) and over.

As their waistlines spread, Americans can take consolation from the fact that most countries are following suit. The rate of obesity in Britain has more than doubled since 1980, according to Tim Gill, secretary of an international task force that studies the subject. On present trends, Britons will overtake Americans by 2020.

WHY DIETS DO NOT WORK

Linda Goodrich

In the following selection, Linda Goodrich explores why women continue to diet when they know that each time they try, they will fail. According to Goodrich, diets simply do not work because they affect the body's functions in ways that hinder weight loss. In addition, she explains, dieting robs the body of the water it needs to function properly, causes changes in the metabolic rate, and can lead to heart irregularities and a variety of other physical problems. Goodrich writes that by dieting, women put their bodies in what she calls "a state of dis-ease." At the same time, she notes, diets affect mental health by causing stress to rise to a level that is not healthy emotionally or physically. Goodrich is a nurse and health and lifestyle counselor.

It seems logical to me that in order to regain control of our bodies, our sizes, our lives, our identities, and to truly empower ourselves as people, we must close the door to the world of diets, body sculpting, and to a culture that is size-based.

The Crazy-Making Diet Roller Coaster

It is my experience that when I used to diet, I always had an initial loss in size. This showed up as weight loss according to the scale. Also, my clothes started to feel bigger on me. And I would fit into some of my smaller-sized clothes that I hadn't been able to wear before the diet. I always got excited, and assumed that finally I had found the right diet. At last, I thought, now I will become happy. How many of us have been there!

I call this the Crazy-Making Diet Roller Coaster. First we go up, and then we go down, as we realize that it is just another diet and it too will fail. As each new attempt to diet fails, we blame ourselves. If only I had more will power, if only I could find the right diet, if only I could find the right pill . . . then I would truly become happy. We all know the heartfelt despair that comes with the realization that this diet, just like all the previous ones, alas has failed!

Reprinted from Linda Goodrich, "Why Diets Don't Work," part 1, Grand Style Women's Club website, http://www.grandstyle.com/goodrich.htm (3/6/98), with permission.

Diets Create a Dis-ease

Psychologists say that it is a sign of lack of intelligence that when people try a solution to a problem and it doesn't work, they keep trying the same approach again and again. So, why do women continue to diet when they know diets don't work? This is a very interesting issue. One would think that it is because basically each diet is somewhat different, and that is the reason that women keep thinking maybe this one will do it. However, it is a generic fault! All diets don't work.

First, let's start with the physical effects diets have on our bodies. The body has its own innate wisdom and consciousness. However, our awareness of this body wisdom has not been fully developed. Most of us find it difficult to retrieve this information. So, for now let's look to the research in the scientific/medical community on dieting to tell us what really happens to our bodies when we are in the dieting pattern.

When we first begin a diet we lose mostly water. This is a very unhealthy state for our bodies to be in. Every system in our bodies needs ample water to function in a healthy way. When water is reduced through dieting, we handicap our systems so that they function much less optimally. In extreme cases we lose precious electrolytes and become dehydrated. This leads to heart irregularities, and a lessening of all of the system's functions.

Another dieting-induced problem is the loss of integrity to the nervous system's stability. We all know this from first hand experience. The irritability that we experience when we stay on a diet for a long period of time can often lead to such intense cravings that we begin to have erratic eating behaviors. You know that the heart is a muscle, and that our bodies' organs are made up of different kinds of muscle that keep us functioning at a healthy level. What happens when we lose weight and it is muscle weight? We are putting our bodies into a state of nutritional insult, and ultimately a state of dis-ease.

Set Points and Yo-Yo Dieting

In reviewing some common knowledge about our bodies and how they operate we find that every body has its own set point or baseline weight, and resists attempts to starve it smaller. As over 95% of all dieters know from firsthand experience, the weight lost comes back plus a few pounds more. In some cases the rebound gain is more than just a few pounds. This is sometimes called the "yo-yo" dieting syndrome. Because the body in its innate wisdom reacts as if there is a famine going on, it lowers the metabolism so as to preserve what is coming in and uses or expends calories at a reduced rate. Fat is stored for future use and heat.

What is even more ironic and frightening to dieters is that the body then resets this "set point" (the point at which it will burn calories) at an even higher rate of intake. Making it that much harder with the next diet to lose and then, to keep off the weight. I'm sure that all of you have heard the phrase, "All I have to do is to look at cake, and it seems that I gain weight." This is the theory of set point at work. With each new diet, your metabolism will require more and more calories to start burning what you eat. This explains why it takes more and more effort to take off weight as years go by and we try more and more restrictive diets. This is why so many compulsive eaters have incorporated exercise into their weight loss goals in hopes of stimulating their metabolism to help lose the pounds. This is one of the many dieting-induced problems.

Dieting Stress

Dieting-induced problems are much more complex and dangerous than merely attempting to change your body's set point, or dealing with rebound weight gain. Each time you go on or off a diet, your body repeatedly has to adjust by changing its metabolic rate. At the same time it must provide sufficient energy to cells and organs. This added burden of requirements places enormous stress upon your body.

A healthy stress level is beneficial to keep us at optimum mental and physical alertness and well being. But the kind of stress created by the diet physiology is of such proportions that it creates an insult to the body's integrity and stability. It is as if we were alternately starved and then showered with abundance. The stress that this puts on our bodies, and the resultant effects are the real causes of a loss of "health." This truly becomes a dis-ease state.

Additionally, when you realize that most women start dieting anywhere between the ages of 8 years old through 13 years, that they do it for 30–40 years or more, it is amazing that we don't get more diseased than we do! The effect on our mental health is of such great impact that many women seem to think that they are going crazy with all the stress of body image, self-esteem and weight.

The loss of self-esteem that is established through repeated failures on diets leads to more complicated mental health issues. The enormous sense of failure related to not "measuring up" to the image of the perfect person the media currently portrays, contributes to the confusion, anger and guilt that every woman (and every man who diets, too) feels about food, eating, and size.

Unrealistic Body Images

Another of the many dieting-induced problems are the severe disordered eating problems that have now become rampant, and in fact, almost epidemic among women. I am speaking specifically about bulimia and anorexia as well as compulsive overeating. These disorders are the results of women trying vainly to model themselves and their bodies after some artists' renditions—most of which are based upon the notions of advertising agencies. These usually are trumped up campaigns to motivate a desire for products for women that promise happiness, sex appeal, and fulfillment.

It is this kind of commercial money-making manipulation that has had women by the throat. We have bought into a scheme to make industry rich—and us, sick! Furthermore, because of our vain attempts to be like the model in the magazine or on the runway, we have each given thousands of dollars to the diet and exercise industry.

Diets make you fat, they help spend your money needlessly, and they keep the fashion and diet/exercise industries rich. They put extreme stress upon your body and help create disease, and they cause you to lose your emotional and mental sense of self. I suppose they do work, if the above results are what you are seeking.

CHAPTER 2

EMOTIONAL HEALTH AND BODY IMAGE

Contemporary Issues
Companion

PROBLEMS WITH BODY IMAGE

Tori DeAngelis

In the following selection, Tori DeAngelis notes that certain myths about body image, such as the belief that only upper-class white women are preoccupied with their appearance, are being shattered by researchers studying how women and men of different ethnic and cultural groups are affected by body-image problems. According to DeAngelis, body-image problems and eating disorders are not unique to any one group; rather, individuals from all groups—males, females, Caucasians, African Americans, heterosexuals, gays, and so on—can be affected. DeAngelis points out that although traditionally women have been the ones most concerned with body image, men have increasingly been experiencing pressure to "look good" and now share many of the same concerns. Tori DeAngelis is on the staff of the *APA Monitor*, the monthly journal of the American Psychological Association.

Upper-class white women are not the only people prone to disliking what they see when they look into the mirror.

More men are worried about their body shape, black women binge-eat as often as white women and lesbians are plagued by their appearance more than stereotypes hold, research shows.

Psychologists believe that a range of factors are feeding the rise in body-image problems in nontraditional groups. One study, for example, shows that advertisements mirror the body-image concerns each gender is most susceptible to. Other research suggests that the reason black women binge-eat is not because their culture accepts heavier weights, but because they're depressed. Such findings emphasize the need for research that examines social, cultural, psychological and personal variables, psychologists say.

Men and Body-Image Problems

While there are no good prevalence studies on men with eating disorders, clinical reports show that about one out of 10 patients with anorexia or bulimia are men. (Women with bulimia make up 4 percent to 5 percent of the population, and women with anorexia make

Reprinted from Tori DeAngelis, "Body Image Problems Affect All Groups," *APA Monitor*, March 1997, by permission. Copyright ©1997 by the American Psychological Association.

up about 1 percent of the population, according to estimates.)

"If you take all kinds of appearance preoccupations—including the desire to be bigger and weigh more, concerns about hair, nose, skin and other parts of the body—you'll find that many more men have body-image problems than you'd think," says James Rosen, PhD, a professor of psychology at the University of Vermont who runs a body-image clinic there.

Research shows that men with eating disorders share a similar psychological profile with women with eating disorders, including a sense of interpersonal ineffectiveness and problems regulating their emotions, psychologists say.

And the same treatments—including cognitive-behavioral therapy and psychotherapy tailored for those with eating disorders—appear to work for both groups, Rosen said.

In a study that examines both body-image concerns and eating disorders in men, Anne Kearney-Cooke, PhD, and Paula Steichen-Ash, PhD, found that men with eating disorders preferred a lean body shape, while men with no eating disorders preferred a V-shaped body, with a strong upper chest and slim waist.

Because men with eating disorders struggle with the same emotional difficulties as their female counterparts, they may be "more vulnerable to the thinness message," Kearney-Cooke suggested—though it's not clear how that dynamic operates in men. . . .

The Role of Advertising

Several studies are examining the suspected role that advertising plays in gender-based body concerns. In a 1992 study in the *International Journal of Eating Disorders*, psychiatrist Arnold Anderson, MD, and Lima DiDomenico, of the University of Iowa, analyzed the number of articles on weight loss and body shape in 10 popular magazines targeted to young men and women.

The women's magazines contained 10.5 times as many advertisements and articles on weight loss as men's, which is consistent with women's tendency to worry about their weight.

(That figure is the same ratio as female to male anorectics, the team noted.)

But men's magazines included more ads that encouraged men to change their body shape by building their upper body and trimming their abdomens, also squaring with Madison Avenue's ideals for men.

Fashion and cologne advertisers are also homing in on men as a new target group, psychologists say.

"Men are feeling as much pressure to look gorgeous as women," says Michael Siever, PhD, a private practitioner in San Francisco who has studied body image in men. "It's as if capitalism woke up and realized there is a lot of money to be made if it urged men to look good."

Other sociocultural variables, such as men's changing economic roles and their shifting roles in relation to women, may explain the rise in men's concerns about their appearance, researchers suggest. However, those factors have not yet been well studied.

The Gay Community

Studies of gay men and lesbians provide another view of the way gender affects body image—and are knocking down myths about lesbians and gay men in the process.

One common stereotype holds that lesbians don't care about their weight and appearance because they are not swayed by society's standards to attract men. Another says that gay men resemble heterosexual women in their obsession with their appearance. But researchers have come to differing conclusions on those points.

In a 1992 study in the *International Journal of Eating Disorders*, University of Vermont researchers Pamela Brand, Esther Rothblum, PhD, and Laura Solomon, PhD, compared lesbians, gay men and heterosexual men and women on weight, dieting, preoccupation with weight and exercise activity.

While heterosexual women and gay men said they were more concerned with their weight than lesbians or heterosexual men, gender was a more salient factor than sexual orientation on most variables, the authors write. Both lesbians and heterosexual women, for instance, reported greater dissatisfaction with their bodies and more dieting than gay or heterosexual men.

The finding suggests that gender-based dictates still significantly affect lesbians' behavior, they note.

A related study in Sex Roles in 1993 found that people overestimate the degree of body-image problems in gay men and heterosexual women.

University of South Florida researchers Thomas E. Gettleman, PhD, and J. Kevin Thompson, PhD, asked 32 gay men, 32 lesbians, 32 heterosexual men and 32 heterosexual women, to describe their own body-image problems, and to take the perspective of a "typical" person in each of the other three groups as well as in the group of which they're a member. . . .

While gay men and heterosexual women reported having more body-image problems than the other two groups, all participants overestimated the degree to which the two stereotyped groups suffered from those disturbances, the team found.

Race and Culture

Psychologist Ruth Striegel-Moore, PhD, is helping to shatter another myth: that black women are immune from eating disorders because they're less worried about having a large body. In a study of 6,000 women, including 1,500 black women, the Wesleyan University psychology professor is finding that black and white women engage in binge-eating behavior at the same rate—about 8 percent for each group. (Engaging in binge-eating is not the same as having the full-blown disorder, Striegel-Moore noted.) The study, funded by the National Institutes of Health, is the largest comprehensive study of eating disorders to include black women. Her preliminary findings also show that both black and white women have the same rates of either bulimia nervosa or binge-eating disorder—3 percent in each group. (She has not yet tested out percentages for each disorder.)

Her data also indicate that black women who binge-eat suffer similar emotional problems that white women do, she said.

No one has adequately studied eating disorders in other ethnic groups such as Hispanics and Asian-Americans, she added.

Women Are Most Affected

While men appear to be plagued by body-image concerns in greater numbers, it's still women who bear the brunt of appearance-oriented ills, psychologists note.

Two recent studies highlight this point. In a meta-analysis of 222 studies conducted over the last 50 years, Yale University psychologist Alan Feingold, PhD, found that the number of women who have a poor body image compared to men rose dramatically from the 1970s on.

The trend was found across a number of body-image measures and descriptors, and wasn't mediated by either self-esteem or actual physical attractiveness, he said. Feingold presented the study as an invited address at the 1996 American Psychological Association (APA) Annual Convention in Toronto.

In another study of 227 college-age men and women . . . , Jennifer Muth and Thomas F. Cash, PhD, of Old Dominion University, found that women had more negative attitudes toward their bodies in three major domains: how they evaluated their own bodies; how much time and activity they spent on their appearance; and how they feel in social situations about their looks.

These data highlight the notion that social prescriptions still negatively rule women's behavior, believes Kelly D. Brownell, PhD, professor of psychology, epidemiology and public health at Yale University.

"If society were in concert with how females actually develop, we'd celebrate the rounding of the female shape around puberty," he said.

"But because women are told to be thin, adolescence signals the onset of a fight with the body that never ends."

WHY THIN IS IN

Jill S. Zimmerman

Jill S. Zimmerman is a psychotherapist in private practice in Evanston, Illinois. She is an expert on body image and lectures extensively on women's issues, including eating disorders and body image. According to Zimmerman, since the late 1800s females of all ages have been sold the belief that thin is beautiful. The media foster and promote this belief, writes Zimmerman, pressuring women and girls to live up to the image projected by beautiful, thin supermodels and movie and television stars. She points out that articles and books describing the diet and exercise strategies of these "ideal" females are everywhere, leading the average woman to believe that she, too, can attain such a thin physique. However, most women and girls will never live up to this image no matter how hard they try, warns Zimmerman; instead, they often end up with poor body image, low self-esteem, and an eating disorder.

She sat there in my office, her delicate face obscured by a shield of blond hair, her timid voice just above a whisper: "I want to look like the supermodels. I'm five-foot-nine, so I have the height, but I can't lose the weight. I'd like to look like Cindy Crawford. But I can't get below 140 pounds." She reminded me of a frightened rabbit as her shaky voice grew even quieter, her eyes softened with tears: "I've tried everything, but I just can't."

Time and time again, I hear this confession in the conversations I have with young women. They want to look good in a bathing suit. They want a tight butt. They go on diets and work out every day. They're never thin enough, so they go to unnatural extremes. All they really want is to feel good about themselves in a sea of doubt and turmoil encouraged by a multi-billion-dollar-a-year beauty industry. And they think the panacea is to look like a supermodel: perfectly thin, tall, sculpted, and commanding—our cultural epitome of feminine success. I have known hundreds of women who feel justified in their starving, binging and purging, and excessive exercise—their attempts to drain themselves of fat and mold their bodies into the illusions of

Excerpted from Jill S. Zimmerman, "An Image to Heal," *The Humanist*, January/February 1997. Reprinted with permission.

perfection that pour into their senses from every direction. Of course, despite the money spent, the sweaty hours on the Stairmaster, the deprivation and abuse, most of these women—like most women everywhere—will never look like supermodels. This cruel reality cuts through them like a poison arrow, causing feelings of anger and shame to flood their unforgiving hearts. Initially, many of my patients don't really have lives; their ideas, feelings, and activities all revolve around calories, fat grams, and numbers on a scale.

When supermodel Cindy Crawford snapped tartly, "Do you look at pictures of me and want to puke?" to the question of whether or not models cause eating disorders, she was not only responding to a coed's provocative question at a Princeton conference. She was broadcasting the viewpoint of the majority of American beauty-industry moguls: focus on the corporate bottom line, and to hell with the health and welfare of those who create the profits. This reckless attitude was reflected by *Harper's Bazaar*'s Tina Gaudoin, who warned in her article, "Body of Evidence," that "models like Kate Moss, Amber Valetta, Nadja Auermann . . . might not [make] you feel good about yourself . . . but this is an ectomorphic body type. It's in fashion. You'll be seeing more of it." I wish every women's magazine editor, advertising executive, cosmetics czar, fitness guru, fashion designer, and modeling agency CEO could have observed my session with the tearful girl who was severely bulimic in her frenzy to get down to Crawford's well-publicized 120 pounds. "Do you look at pictures of me and want to puke?" Evidently they're not hearing—or paying attention to—a deafening "Yes!" from the seven million American girls and women who, according to Dr. Vivian Meehan, president of Anorexia Nervosa and Associated Disorders, suffer from eating disorders. (Add to this the number of male youths who struggle with society's image of the perfect stud and with eating disorders.) . . .

A Historical Perspective

The idea that we can—and should—accept our natural body types is a relatively new concept. For over a century, newspapers and magazines have been deluging Americans with images of ideal beauty, and only strict emulation of these ideals has been sanctioned as attractive. There was a period of time during the early- to mid-1800s when the full feminine figure was considered beautiful. However, the slimmer, more athletic-looking Gibson Girl, first created by artist Charles Dana Gibson, replaced it as the ideal in the 1890s, and thinness has remained an integral part of female attractiveness ever since. (Thinness, of course, is always relative. According to the August 1905 *Ladies Home Journal*, the Gibson girl had average measurements of 38-27-45—quite chunky by today's standards.)

The Gibson Girl remained the image of American beauty until World War I, when the flapper became the vanguard of fashionableness, prompting the late Dr. Morris Fishbein, longtime editor of the *Journal of the American Medical Association*, to lament, "Of all the fads which have affected mankind, none seems more difficult to explain than the desire of American women for the barberpole figure." During the Great Depression of the 1930s, the flapper lost her popularity; larger, stronger, more mature ideals superseded her "boyish form" during this time of national hardship. But after World War II, at the start of the baby boom, women's magazines began promoting Christian Dior's "New Look," which demanded a hand-span waist—and the necessary corsets, girdles, waist cinches, and diets to achieve it. With Audrey Hepburn—like models as the new embodiments of haute couture, women once again felt too fat.

Women's magazines have had no mercy on teenagers who, for generations, have been encouraged to join their mothers in worrying about their weight. According to *Seventeen*, Carol Lynley, the first celebrity teen model, "came prepared for every photo shoot in the 1950s with a head of lettuce, a pound of seedless grapes, and three green peppers," her food for the day. In the 1960s, *Mademoiselle* and *Seventeen* became saturated with columns and features enumerating the diet strategies and exercise habits of models—a practice that continues to this day.

The 1960s

Starting in 1962 with "How to Look Like a *Seventeen* Model," young women learned that even a model as slim as Susan Van Wyck (at 32-20-33) was told to lose 10 pounds at the beginning of her career. Van Wyck told teens, "It was agony dieting . . . because I love to eat. But I finally made it!" Other popular models shared their secrets with eager readers, such as this tidbit from that much adored prom-queenesque brunette Colleen Corby: "Even though I love pork chops and steak . . . I've been eating lots of fish . . . and seafoods [which] are low in calories." In "Do You Want to Be a Model?" modeling agency fixture Eileen Ford informed readers that an average model was five feet, seven inches, and between 100 and 115 pounds, and that one of the most indispensable items in a model's tote bag was "a waist cinch that really pulls you in around the middle" to make the "typical 20-22" waist look even smaller. *Mademoiselle*'s "How Beautiful Can You Get?" depicted the dramatic makeover of an aspiring model: Barbara Gallant dieted down to 100 pounds, had a nose job, dyed her hair blond, had corrective braces on her teeth, and received localized dehydration treatment to smooth out her hips and thighs—"thoroughly remodeled so she could become a model!"

Perhaps the only 1960s model who reportedly didn't have to jump through diet and exercise hoops to keep her slender figure was also the skinniest: Twiggy, the icon of Mod at five feet, six inches, and 89 pounds. She admitted to eating "anything, absolute rubbish," including the ice cream and chocolate sauce *piece de resistance* "Bananas Twiggy" whipped up especially for her at her favorite London restaurant. Her irreverent eating habits aside, Twiggy set a standard that most models found impossible to reach. In his book *Models*, Michael Gross quotes Gillian Bobroff, a British model in the 1960s, as saying, "It was dreadful. . . . [Twiggy] started a trend, and you had to be just the same. I . . . started killing myself, taking a million slimming pills. I never ate. I had bulimia. It was a nightmare, trying to keep up."

The 1970s and 1980s

Even though the 1970s brought us larger, more healthy-looking images, models still had to diet with Herculean effort to keep their shapes. Cheryl Tiegs, the most highly paid model of that decade, wrote *The Way to Natural Beauty*, which became a hot seller among young women in 1980. At five feet, ten inches, and 120 pounds, Tiegs offered a variety of dieting tips, including:

> Weigh in every morning. As soon as you've gained a pound, cut back on your food consumption. . . . I don't let another morsel pass my lips after 6:00 PM. . . . I always ask the waiter not to serve me potatoes, rolls, or creamed vegetables if they come with a meal. When I need to drop a pound in a big hurry, I skip dinner, breakfast, and lunch the next day and eat a small dinner the following evening.

Tiegs also gave some interesting advice on how to start a diet, which likely reflected her own ambivalence toward such a limited regimen: "Before you go on a serious diet, I recommend that you eat all the food you can manage for three solid days. The point is to overdo it, knowing that you will never overeat again."

Model/actress Brooke Shields, touted by designer Calvin Klein in the 1980s as being "the most beautiful girl in the world" came out with her own book, *On Your Own*, in 1985. A model since she was a baby, Shields, now in her early thirties, admits that she has dieted since she was eight, when she "decided to give up soda pop and pizza." In *On Your Own*, she confesses, "I have to diet constantly to keep my weight down" and shares her appetite-squelching bag of tricks, such as eating half a grapefruit and drinking a glass of warm lemon water one-half hour before meals. She is apparently scared to death of her sweet-tooth: "Do whatever you have to do not to indulge in . . . sweets. Run in place, do sit-ups, sit on your hands—but don't eat those cookies!"

To Kim Alexis, one of the most sought-after models of the 1980s, looking back on a hugely successful modeling career revives some especially painful memories. She told *People:*

> I remember trying every fad diet . . . starving myself for four days in a row. I remember trying the Atkins diet, which was

low carbohydrate, high protein. If I didn't drop 10 pounds in a week, I was on to another diet. I think I was a normal person before I started screwing around with all these diets. My metabolism got screwed up. I lost my period. . . . I cried for the first year of my career.

Now in her mid-thirties, Alexis admits that she's suffered "long-term health effects from the crazy diets." Today she eats healthy, low-fat meals and insists, "I'm a big, strong girl." The only apparent residue from her model dieting mentality is that she reportedly takes CitriMax, a natural appetite suppressant that she has also endorsed.

The 1990s

Supermodels may be enjoying a bigger piece of the beauty-industry pie in the 1990s, but the standards by which they are judged by agents and clients have also escalated. They must model fashions that, according to *Vogue*'s May 1995 "Point of View," "demand a body at its personal peak. Hard work is one way to get there; counting calories is another. . . . A well-honed physique is worth any price." According to *Shape* magazine, "Agencies are asking their models to get strong, lean, and more defined. A little bit of extra weight . . . could hurt [their] photographic images or their ability to fit into the narrow cut of couture clothes. Agencies give these women a matter of weeks to shape up, tone down, or ship out." And most models must jump to the command or risk losing financial security.

Consequently, it's hardly surprising that we sometimes stumble upon magazine articles such as *Vogue*'s "Nobody's Perfect," which disseminate a body-image message with a twist: even supermodels feel heaped with physical flaws and are slaves to their self-perpetuated myths. To the cynical, this could be construed as a marketing ploy to promote an even stronger identification between the average woman and the supermodel. But through my work with eating-disordered women, I've learned that models aren't invincible to poor body image.

An ironic example of this is Cindy Crawford. On the one hand, she's flippant in her attitude about models' impacts on eating disorders, on the other, her colleagues apparently affect her in much the same way that she affects my bulimic patient. For in spite of being acknowledged as a world-class beauty, Crawford admitted to *Vogue* that she felt "self-conscious of my arms, because I look at someone like Linda [Evangelista] and she has these little bird arms and they look great in clothes." Crawford also doesn't like the area right under her butt, "where the cellulite tends to come," and thinks that her feet are too wide. Evangelista, in turn, told interviewers that she covets Christy Turlington's mouth and would like to "remove two ribs—or just shrink the size of my rib cage."

Nadja Auermann, who "eats like a horse" (according to Tina Gaudoin) and who lost half her body weight before becoming a super-model (according to the 1994 *Vogue* article "Platinum Hit") reportedly still has high anxiety about her weight. Auermann attributes this to her early experiences as a model in Paris: "Everybody made me para-noid. Everybody told me, 'Nadja, you can't eat so much. You have to stop.' If I gained half a gram, I was like completely freaking out."

Glamour reported that supermodel Tyra Banks once canceled a job because of a "bloated stomach" and often thinks about holding in her stomach during shoots. *Top Model*, a magazine devoted to the promo-tion of models, disclosed that Victoria Secret's Stephanie Seymour—at five feet, nine inches, with perfect supermodel measurements of 34-24-34—"thinks she's too fat and hates her buttocks." And Christy Turlington, my 19-year-old neighbor's favorite model and the star of Calvin Klein's recent underwear ads, told *Vogue* she had considered cosmetic surgery at one point: "I don't like my knees. . . . I hate my feet, they're just big and long and skinny. . . . I have a beer belly." She concurs with Auermann that "fashion editors can be very cruel. . . . They constantly watch you and say, 'Oh, look at your ass.' They do that all the time." Indeed, to highlight the plight of her fellow super-models, Carol Alt was quoted in *People* as saying, "Anyone who thinks that society pressures women to live up to our image should think of what we have to go through to maintain that image." It's true: super-models are ensnared with the rest of women in the sticky web of nev-er feeling thin enough, of lacking the inner security of body accep-tance. A supermodel's toil may culminate in a fabulous career, but the cost is often a well of inner unhappiness.

But the legacy lives on. Articles and books proclaiming the strenuous diets and work-out schedules of models—1990s' style—are ubiquitous in bookstores, on newsstands, and in grocery store checkout lines. . . .

How Stars Fight Fat

Actresses also deserve some recognition for the suffering intrinsic to their profession. Like models, they're under the gun. If they're consid-ered fat and unfit, they're considered unattractive—which spells fail-ure in a field overflowing with one "perfect"-looking woman after another. According to an article in *Longevity*, Pamela Anderson Lee had a contract with *Baywatch* that strictly forbade her to gain weight. The article says that Anderson Lee "follows a mind-boggling fitness regi-men. Even during non-working months, Anderson keeps to a rigorous program of 25-mile mountain bike rides or one- to two-hour athletic walks, plus 50 lap pool swims or more strenuous ocean swims."

The *Redbook* article "Take It Off Like a Star" described Oprah Win-frey as having "a maniac exercise routine" that includes two daily four-mile runs, plus 45 minutes on the Stairmaster and 350 sit-ups. The article reported, "In an eight-month period, [Winfrey] walked, climbed, biked, and hiked about 2,260 miles—the distance from her own Harpo Studios in Chicago to Eureka, California." Bette Midler reportedly eats nothing but vegetables after 5:00 pm. Demi Moore's workout "stresses crosstraining: road cycling, ocean and river kayaking, snowshoeing, hiking, skiing, plus daily weight lifting." Moore, like many stars, has a live-in nutritionist/cook and a personal trainer to ensure that she adheres to her strenuous workout schedule and spa cuisine. (Would we really trade places with any of them if we had to live in fear of losing our jobs if we gained five pounds?)

In the schizophrenic 1990s, women's magazines routinely show two sides of the same coin: a gooey, fat-laden chocolate cake recipe placed next to an advertisement for Slimfast; "How the Stars Fight Fat" diet tips across the page from an article on anorexia nervosa. It is not often that women's magazines present articles that are actually meaningful for today's body-image-conflicted woman. . . .

In 1980, *Seventeen* published a groundbreaking article, written by a teenager, on the media's effect on body image. In "Let's Become Our Own Best Friend!" Lisanne L. Renner stated:

> Physical appearance plays an important role in our emotional development. Hollywood makes us feel inadequate if our bodies aren't carbon copies of the professional beauties seen in movies or on television. We seem to be so busy wishing our figures were a perfect size five that we forget there is beauty in individuality. . . . Next time you look into a mirror, don't dwell on the negative. Instead, compliment yourself!

Apparently, her important advice went unheeded. In 1984, a *Glamour* survey revealed that, out of 33,000 female respondents, 85 percent felt dissatisfied with their bodies. This statistic has not improved over the years, most girls and women of the 1990s continue to be plagued by poor body image. . . .

Fighting Back

All women—rich or poor, thin or fat, famous or not—can be caught up in poor body image and low self-esteem. It is important that we find ways to disentangle ourselves from that web. We must wriggle free before we can learn to really feel good about ourselves, body type and all. In doing so, we need to make friends with all our parts—our desire to be healthy and fit, our desire for friendship, our desire for the intimacy of a significant other, our desire to inhabit a peaceful mind, our desire for a successful career, our desire to look attractive, our desire to raise happy children, our desire to be creative, and so forth—so that, instead of hating the roll of fat under our buttocks or wishing our tummies were hollowed in, we can accept who we are and revel in that. Most of us would agree intellectually that diversity in bodies is as natural and acceptable as diversity in flowers or trees. We must learn to embrace this idea with our emotions and our spirits as well. For as Brooke Shields fights her war against cookies, she is really waging a war against her body. If she—if we—could only learn that eating cookies is one of our rightful choices, cookies would lose their power to punish us. Cookies would be on our side. We may choose to eat them (and there is nothing wrong with that), we may choose to wrap them up and give them to a friend, we may choose to save them for later or to throw them in the garbage. . . .

Are we too intimidated to change? Are we too scared to look the media bullies in the eye and say, "No!"? Angela Farmer, an internationally renowned yoga instructor, was once asked by a student, "Why can't I do this pose?" Farmer replied, "You must soften your buttocks—that is, of course, unless you're afraid of losing a tight bottom" The quality of our lives would so greatly improve if we could only believe that a hard body isn't the only kind of attractive body and that having some softness and looseness may actually be beneficial to our health and beauty. (To look at Angela Farmer verifies this as fact.)

But how do we work on our self-image? How do we change our thinking and feeling habits in order to unite our various parts and neutralize the negativity that our culture blasts our way via the media? Unfortunately, we can't wave a magic wand to make our culture more sensitive to our needs. But we can change our own attitudes: we can refuse to take the media so seriously and we can challenge the images and their devaluing messages. The only way our culture will change is if we stop believing in the social attitudes which make us feel not good enough and start believing in ourselves and our right to *our* individual body—even if it isn't a body type currently worshipped as fashionable.

A Positive Self-Image

Young women like Natalie Laughlin are leading the way. A plus-size model, she represents an alternative and has learned to feel good about herself even though she's not a size four. In a 1995 *Glamour* article, she states, "I don't restrict myself to certain styles and colors. The other night I wore a black velvet turtleneck bodysuit with a form-fitting sarong skirt—but I'm just as likely to wear red chiffon. Now when I work out, it's not about losing weight . . . it's about feeling better, feeling my own strength. I no longer base my worth on what my body looks like. I'm making peace with it."

Others are following in Laughlin's footsteps. Mandi Patterson describes herself as an overweight teen who is learning to value herself. In an essay published in *Parade*, she wrote: "I've been fat all my life. I've made a vow to lose weight . . . but I don't think I can reach my goals when I'm constantly feeling ugly and self-conscious. I'm learning to accept myself the way I am and to respect myself, even though I have a weight problem."

Nineteen-year-old Susanna isn't overweight but nonetheless has been deeply affected by media stereotypes. She shared these thoughts with me in a casual interview:

> I think there's a direct link between the models who are the most popular and girls feeling bad about their bodies. Almost everyone I knew in high school, except for me, had an eating disorder. I'm serious. I think the reason they felt like they had to lose weight is that the media portrays women having these perfect bodies. They aren't realistic. So girls feel they need to weigh less. This year I've gained 20 pounds and it looks different and I have to get used to that. I mean I really was like a waif, and now I'm more athletic. That's how I want to be. I don't want to be unhealthy.

In another conversation, Kate, age 12, pointing to a picture in a magazine, put it this way:

> I like the sweater on this model and she's not a supermodel. She doesn't starve herself, you can just tell. I'd be happy with that. That should be the kind of model that people should put in magazines, because it's just getting out of hand with people not eating. The models aren't eating, and girls look at them and think, "Look how pretty they are. Look how skinny they are. Maybe if I don't eat and I wear those clothes, I'll look just like them." Girls won't eat and then they make themselves throw up. I had a friend last year who stopped eating for a while because she thought she was too fat. But she really wasn't.

These young women are only a few examples of the many sensitive thinkers—young and old—who have begun to give media images a critical look. For all of us women—whether were students, homemakers, lawyers, heart surgeons, or supermodels—are wounded warriors. We've been in the trenches fighting a war against our bodies for generations. Our healing has something to do with mending ourselves so that the wounded places can grow stronger, so that we have energy to cultivate the gardens that are ourselves.

WHY PEOPLE OVEREAT

Michelle Joy Levine

A certified psychotherapist and psychoanalyst, Michelle Joy Levine is a faculty member at the Society for Psychoanalytic Study and Research in New York. In the following selection from her book *I Wish I Were Thin . . . I Wish I Were Fat*, Levine writes about the real reasons people overeat. There are conscious and obvious reasons for compulsive overeating, Levine notes, such as using food as a reward. She stresses, however, that compulsive overeating also stems from unconscious wishes, fears, and conflicts. According to Levine, people who compulsively overeat may be using food to lessen the anxiety produced by these underlying conflicts. Because these reasons are hidden in the unconscious, she explains, most compulsive overeaters are not aware of what keeps them from controlling their eating behaviors.

I have been on a diet for as long as I can remember, at least since I was five years old. My mother put me on a diet then because she said I was getting too fat. I imagine because she was obese, she wanted to make sure I wouldn't be. But looking back at childhood pictures, I was never really fat as a child. When I was about five years old, you might say I still had some baby fat, but you would never describe me as being fat. If I must say so myself, I was kind of cute. Nevertheless my mother told me I had to diet and, therefore I could not have more than one cookie from the box of assorted cookies placed in front of me at the kitchen table. Sometimes, when my mother wasn't looking, I would sneak another cookie. When I was six or seven years old, I remember stealing money from my mother's handbag to buy chocolate covered halvah from the local grocery. It cost three cents and I could get three of them if I stole a dime. I still feel as if I am sneaking food when I eat something I love. And sometimes I still feel guilty when I let it get the better of me: when I eat too much of something delicious. My present desire to eat what I shouldn't probably stems from those experiences. Although I know I am not really fat, I still often think and feel I am. I have worried about how fat I am since I was a little girl. *And I have been dieting ever since.*

I am a psychotherapist in the private practice of treating adults and adolescents. Since going into the field of psychology, I have spent a lot of time thinking about why people overeat. Why were my mother, her sister and brother obese? Why do people spend millions of dollars on one diet book or program after another to lose weight? Why do the people who finally lose the weight regain those pounds, plus more?

There are many conscious and obvious reasons we overeat. Eating is pleasurable. Overeating can provide pleasure when we are not getting enough joy out of life. When things are not going well, a hot fudge sundae may make us feel better. Chinese food or Raisinettes do the trick for me. Many people forget their pain or troubles and feel better while they are eating something delicious. Just think how many children are offered an ice cream cone when they fall down and cry. Many parents do what their parents did. They offer something delicious to soothe the hurt. For most of us, soothing pain with something delicious begins very early in life.

I grew up in one of the thousands of apartment buildings in congested Brooklyn, New York. But one summer, when I was seven, we went to "the country." I felt free wandering gleefully around in the woods. It was wonderful. But my joy soon ended. I tripped and fell in the woods and got pebbles in my knee. I remember it as if it were yesterday, though it was decades ago. I ran to my mother crying hysterically and pointing to my bleeding knee. My mother looked down at my bloody knee and then at me. In an attempt to soothe and calm me, she said if I let her take the pebbles out of my knee she would take me to the candy store and I could have anything I wanted. This was extraordinary. I was, after all, the little girl who couldn't even have more than one cookie. Since I knew I was not going to have a choice about having the pebbles taken out of my knee, I made the deal. Picking out all my favorite candies was fantastic. But eating them with my mother there and approving, was ecstasy. Going to the doctor usually brought the same reward: something delicious to eat. It feels childish to admit, but even today, it is difficult for me to go to the doctor or do something else which is painful without rewarding myself with some candy. The desire to soothe or reward myself with candy is still with me some forty odd years later.

Food Is Love, Fun, and Intimacy

James Coco, the actor, says he was a skinny child until he was nine years old. He points to his tonsillectomy as the beginning of his weight problem. "Without that tonsillectomy, I might never have had a weight problem. Though I was terrified at first of surgery, my parents won me over by describing the ice cream feast to come. . . . Visions of Breyer's hand-dipped ice cream danced in my head as I went under the anesthetic—vanilla, chocolate, strawberry, the three main flavors they made then. My last conscious thought was of chocolate." Mr.

Coco acknowledges that of course there were other reasons for his overeating. One, he states, is that to him "Food is love."

Overeating can be fun, especially with others. Think about it. What do most people do when they get together? They eat. They eat brunch. They eat lunch. They eat dinner. They eat après dinner. What do we think of when we get together for Easter, Passover, Christmas, Thanksgiving, etc.? What are we going to eat? For weeks ahead of time we plan what we will cook, prepare or eat for our holiday dinners. It has been that way probably since the beginning of time. We celebrate by eating. Eating is how we share a good time and pleasure with others. It is a way of connecting. It is a pleasure both to the senses and to the emotions.

Recently my son had a slumber party. My husband and I understood perfectly when he gave us the long list of "munchies" to buy for the party. For my son and his friends, the best part of the party was eating all the "junk" food they possibly could. Throwing it at each other was an additional delight.

A man I know feared he might have diabetes. Medically he had reason for his fear. We talked about the possibility this fear was related to his mother and father developing adult onset diabetes. But his biggest fear was not that he might have a serious, possibly life threatening disease. His fear was if he did indeed have diabetes, it would prevent him from having desserts. I found that hard to believe. But he said, "Really, I'm serious. One of the biggest pleasures I have in life is sharing desserts with my wife at the end of dinner. It's a big part of our intimacy and fun."

Now with greater public awareness of health issues, we know overeating, fat, cholesterol and sugar are all bad for us. If you eavesdrop on conversations, you can overhear friends relating stories of how they try to trick themselves out of eating all those wonderful, but, alas, bad foods. I, myself, have shared stories with friends about freezing desserts so that I wouldn't eat them, only to discover, when I weakened, that some frozen cakes are even better than fresh cake! One comedian jokes about avoiding the temptation of fattening foods by throwing them away. However, an hour later she finds herself rummaging through her garbage retrieving the forbidden food, brushing it off and eating it. The audience laughs. The audience connects. Often, when we are not eating, we are joking and talking about food. We identify and we connect through food.

Eating to Overcome Emotions

Overeating, like smoking or drinking, helps divert some people from feelings of anxiety. When something is going wrong, the first thing overeaters think about is eating. Eating, or more drastically, bingeing, helps assuage the upsetting feelings for the moment. Like when my mother took the pebbles out of my knee, even though it hurt, the hurt is softened by being nurtured. Eating is something we do to divert our attention away from an emotion, even a positive one, that is so intense it doesn't feel comfortable.

Little is said about eating when there is an intense positive emotion. My desire to write this book [*I Wish I Were Thin . . . I Wish I Were Fat*] raised some doubts. I believed it was such an important book; how was it possible no one has written it before? I did a lot of research, reading many books and journal articles about overeating and eating disorders. But in all my research I did not find any book that suggested what I wished to communicate. When I was in the library the last time and realized no one else had written this kind of book, I became extremely excited that writing this book was becoming a very real possibility. It would be a dream come true to write a book helping people to understand the powerful underlying wishes and fears that cause us to overeat. I was so excited I didn't know what to do with myself.

At first what I wanted to do was eat and eat a lot. I was not hungry, but that very excited feeling, which was lasting a long time, began to feel very uncomfortable. Eating would be a way to calm myself a little, (I did not want to lose all of the excitement, but just quiet it a little.) I wanted to mollify the pleasurable and happy, but too intense, feeling of excitement. Ironically, here I was thinking about writing a book about overeating, and precisely at that moment what I was thinking about doing was overeating! Ultimately I told my husband about it, who laughed and shared in the excitement. That, plus beginning to write, was what helped.

Even pleasurable feelings can be uncomfortable. Many people, especially those who do not overeat, would react in the exact opposite way. They would be unable to eat. But overeaters typically rely on food to deal with many things.

A Sense of Shame

For many, one of the most gratifying pleasures in the world is eating. But not all people overeat. It is incomprehensible to someone who overeats, that a person can eat a little of something delicious and not want any more, because he has had enough. When we overeat with a person like that, we feel ashamed of overeating. Intuitively we know there is another reason we are eating too much. Often this shame brings about hiding of, or even self deception about, eating.

My obese mother used to tell my sister and me that she just could not lose weight. She would tell us how she watched what she ate very carefully, but her body would not comply. Growing up, I felt so badly for her. The shame of her weight affected her whole life. When I was about twelve years old, I found out why she could not lose weight. I was babysitting my younger sister when my mother went out one evening. We both were hungry, so I decided to cook something for us. I went looking in the "pot closets" for the proper pot to make soup.

Lo and behold, behind the pots, all kinds of goodies were hidden. There was a large assortment of candy and cake, things my mother *never* ate openly. Her shame at not being able to resist overeating sweets obviously caused my mother to lie to us and maybe to herself.

Despite these conscious and obvious reasons for overeating, the most compelling reason people overeat is less obvious. Overeating has more to do with *unconscious wishes and fears* than anything else. Truly! Even though you are certain you want to be thin, if you are consistently overeating, unconscious wishes and fears of being thin most likely exist. . . .

The Conscious and the Unconscious

When an individual consistently or compulsively overeats, invariably that overeating is unconsciously and symbolically representing something other than just eating. People who overeat may believe their greatest wish is to be thin. But if they are overeating, unconsciously they have other wishes which are even more powerful than their wish to be thin. Overeating may represent an unconscious wish to be fat or a fear of being thin. . . . The most important and driving forces underlying overeating are our unconscious wishes and fears. Anyone who consistently overeats does so because of an unconscious wish or fear related to eating or being fat. These wishes and fears are so powerful that the most rigorous dieting is defeated because of them. . . .

Essentially, to successfully lose weight and keep it off, we have to change our diets to include mostly low fat foods and we must exercise. But again *most importantly,* we must resolve the conscious and unconscious wishes we have to be fat.

A truly sad story attests to that fact. Michael Hebranko, a forty-three-year-old man had to have his living room bay window, shrubs and part of an aluminum fence from his front yard removed so that he could be lifted by fork lift and taken to the hospital in a specially constructed ambulance to treat his pneumonia, heart disease, gangrene, fluid in his lungs and collapsed veins. You see, Mr. Hebranko weighs about 940 pounds and could not fit through his front door. The tragedy of Mr. Hebranko's story does not end there. In 1993, Mr. Hebranko was listed in the *Guinness Book of Records* for losing the greatest amount of weight in the shortest period of time. He lost 705 pounds in eighteen months. When asked by reporters why he allowed himself to regain 735 pounds, he was reported as saying, "I took care of the outside problem instead of the inside one."

It is not fun to be overweight. Overweight people are frequently regarded as having emotional problems. In fact, several of my patients have said the greatest shame about their weight is being thought of as emotionally inferior. The overweight are definitely stigmatized. . . .

In the biography *Oprah!*, by Robert Waldron, Oprah Winfrey is quoted about her struggle with overeating. She said when people told her to use will power and just close her mouth, she felt like slapping them. For her and many others, control over eating is very difficult and often even impossible.

Many people think the overweight have no control over themselves. They regard them as weak and lacking in will power. Actually overeaters are not any weaker than anyone else. In addition to possible conscious conflicts, people who are significantly overweight harbor unconscious wishes or fears related to eating. That is the reason they are not in control of their overeating. . . .

A "Compromise Solution"

Sometimes an unconscious wish may conflict with another unconscious wish. Or an unconscious wish may conflict with a conscious wish. . . .

When our wishes are in conflict, our egos find a way to deal with the conflict in the least anxiety provoking way possible. In psychoanalytic terms this resolution is called a "compromise solution.". . .

For the overeater, more often than not, the compromise solution is to be fat. *As outrageous as it may sound, the solution that results in the least amount of anxiety is to overeat and look fat.* Of course this solution is not usually what is consciously experienced. In fact consciously, the person may be feeling a great deal of anxiety about being overweight. If you ask an overweight woman (or man) what his or her wish would be if granted the three proverbial wishes by a fairy godmother, it would not be uncommon for the answer to be an immediate "Of course, to be thin." However, if this person is overeating, a different, unconscious wish is prevailing. Clearly then, overeating is the compromise that brings about the least possible pain or anxiety. That does not mean that overeating eliminates anxiety. It usually does not. What it does mean is, that given all the person's conscious and unconscious wishes, the behavior that results in the least anxiety and discomfort is overeating. Truly, being thin may result in even greater anxiety for the overeater.

Cara, a thirty-six year old obese woman, noticed her reflection in a store window and was appalled. She felt repulsed by what she saw. She usually avoided mirrors, so this reflection was startling. She thought, "That's it, I'm going on a strict diet." She had a glimmer of her unconscious wish, however, when she subsequently thought, "Maybe not. At least I'm safe this way." Her conscious wish was not to look fat. However her unconscious wish, the one that wins out over and over, was "I want to be fat because it keeps me safe." Why being fat allows some people to feel safe will become clearer as we go on.

The kind of obesity I am addressing is due to overeating. I am not referring to people who, due to their genetic inheritance, energy use or other physiological factors, maintain more body weight than they wish.

Unconscious wishes are so powerful they exert tremendous control over all our behavior. The conscious wish of the person who wants to be thin is not to overeat. The unconscious wish of the person who overeats, however, is so powerful, that despite the strength of the conscious wish, there is tremendous difficulty controlling overeating. People who overeat know this intuitively. They know there is something else causing their lack of control over eating. However, since it is unconscious, they are unaware of what it is. They cannot understand why their eating is out of control. They end up feeling weak, inadequate and ashamed. . . .

Unconscious wishes and fears significantly influence overeating. Bulimia and Anorexia Nervosa are eating disorders based on unconscious, as well as conscious conflicts, wishes and fears. Consistent overeating is also based on unconscious as well as conscious conflicts, wishes and fears.

A WAY OF COPING

Kathryn J. Zerbe

Kathryn J. Zerbe is the Jack Aron Professor of Psychiatric Education and a training psychoanalyst at the Menninger Clinic in
Topeka, Kansas. The following selection is taken from her book,
*The Body Betrayed: A Deeper Understanding of Women, Eating Disor-
ders, and Treatment.* Zerbe explains that people with eating disorders use them as a way of coping with situations or emotions
they cannot avoid, such as sadness or poor self-esteem. She notes
that even if these people recognize that their eating disorder is
"self-defeating and dangerous," they believe that they need it to
survive. According to Zerbe, a person with an eating disorder will
continue to rely on the disorder until he or she recognizes what
the real problem is and can develop new coping skills to deal
with it.

An eating disorder can itself be considered a coping strategy par excel-
lence. Viewing it this way helps us see how the symptoms have been
used to adapt to internal and external difficulties. At first blush, eating
disorders may appear destructive and hurtful (as indeed they are), but
they also serve less apparent functions. Patients who have revealed
their struggles with these disorders often talk about how they used the
eating disorder to cope with personal burdens. . . .

A high number of patients (at least 30%) do not recover easily
despite active treatment for their eating disorder. Studies show that
another 30% improve without attaining the highest level of functioning either they or their treaters would like to see. Meanwhile, they are
painfully aware that their eating disorder is hurting them, sapping
their energy, and contributing to their sense of personal failure. Why
is it, then, that these individuals cannot easily give up the eating disorder when other choices seem so apparent?

For most people, the symptom persists because it provides at least
one (and probably more) ways of coping. As Boris wrote about treating patients with eating disorders, "What we [therapists and family
members] call their symptoms, they call their salvation." This "salvation" provided by bulimia or anorexia implies a nearly religious devo-

tion these patients have to holding on to their symptoms. . . .

Eating disorders are ultimately self-defeating and dangerous, but their beguiling feature is that they appear essential to survival, even as they threaten it. Ultimately, the individual clings to the eating disorder to avoid something worse. It is only as the person recognizes what that "something worse" is and finds new and more adaptive ways of coping that she can be free to make the choice to give up the symptoms. In essence, she must find some other salvation—that is, she must develop new coping skills, such as creativity, assertiveness, and enjoyment of hobbies and interpersonal relationships. . . .

From the outset, I must stress that I am suggesting only a partial understanding of and purpose underlying the meaning of eating disorders. I have learned from my patients and their families that each woman has a unique story to tell; the many reasons for their eating disorders are complex and always quite different. They have relied on their eating disorders for novel reasons that have sometimes shifted over the course of their own lives. Thus, my patients have taught me more than any textbook about how efficiently and effectively an eating disorder can help someone deal with loss, sadness, abuse, poor self-esteem, abandonment, and sexual conflict. . . .

The Terror of Needs

Most of us have experienced certain distressing and discomforting feelings. Whether we feel demoralized, angry, depressed, or anxious, we need to safely discharge these emotions somehow. But handling them constructively is a challenging task, especially when we are not aware of what is bothering us.

Although such dilemmas plague everybody, it is always easier to recognize the problem of misdirected emotions in somebody else rather than ourselves. From earliest infancy, we tend to rid ourselves of bad, painful feelings by projecting them out into the world or onto another person, usually our mother or primary caretaker, who can effectively and compassionately contain them.

Because young children do not yet have the internal reservoir to handle their feelings alone, the expectation is that our mothers will be able to reflect these feelings back to us in more manageable doses. Meanwhile, just as children need to get rid of what is bad, they also try to take in, or introject, what is good. Under the best of circumstances, loving and empathic parents or parental substitutes help children learn that their needs are acceptable and can be gratified by the environment.

Naturally, not all our needs can be met, perhaps because our constitutional or hereditary endowment places undue stress on the mother. Sometimes she cannot handle her child's needs—either because she is gong through a stressful period herself or is just unable to intuitively match the child's urgent demands. As a consequence, the child

begins to experience the world as unable to meet its basic requirements. Instead, the world seems abandoning, attacking, persecutory,
and cruel. Whenever legitimate imperatives for nurturance are not
met, such children develop the view that those very necessities are
inordinately wrong. They may blame themselves for having needs; or
they may feel damned and relegated to a world that persecutes them
for their demands, which can cause self-hatred to develop.

One outcome of this dilemma is a defensive strategy in which the
individual gives up on having her needs met. In effect, she says to
everyone in her life, "I don't need anyone. I don't even need food." In
this scenario, food becomes a symbol of persecution. At other times
food may be used temporarily, like a drug, to dull the sensation of
persecution through bingeing, only to be gotten rid of when the individual feels satiated or bloated. Purging becomes an ingenious way of
getting rid of the internal persecutor, just as starving is a way to control the persecutor by not taking anything in.

In one scenario, the child senses that her parents have difficulty
understanding and attuning themselves to her. Because their original
message may have been that her needs were inordinate and unman-
ageable, the eating disorder patient now strives to control those
needs. If no one can meet them, the patient will try to control them
herself. As a result, a false sense of self-sufficiency causes the patient
to do all she can to keep her distance both from food and from other
people. To risk acknowledging one's needs for another person means
handing over an inordinate amount of control and power. It implies
dependence by indicating that the other person is important to the
self, a possibility that can be frightening to anyone who has not
found others to be soothing or kind. The perceived dependence
invites attack or persecution, as the following case vignette illustrates.

> Samantha O. was a 40-year-old mother of three who was
> making considerable headway in the treatment of her 12-year
> struggle with anorexia nervosa. Subjected to severe parental
> neglect as a girl, Samantha longed for intense interpersonal
> relationships that would give her some of the parental care
> and concern she had not received as a small child.
>
> Her expectations in relationships were always dashed, howev-
> er, because no one could meet her demands. Samantha ended
> up hating herself for resenting other people's successes and
> their capacity to make commitments. By refusing to eat,
> Samantha tried to show people that she could get along with-
> out whatever they had to offer. Much as she wanted to be
> nurtured, she fought it in the form of refusing sustenance,
> because eating made her feel all the more deficient and aware
> of what she really coveted. . . .

It is important for family members, therapists, and friends to be aware that generosity may be particularly aversive to the individual with an eating disorder. It incites envy, because she feels so unable to give anything herself. She must then attempt to show others up, to deflate the value of those who seem to have more than she has. The anorexic patient, in particular, wants people to see her as self-sufficient. Her refusal to eat signals to others that they should want what she has and what she can do by refusing food, so that she becomes the object of envy herself. Her symptoms also vividly indicate that others have nothing she wants or needs, and thus they are not to be envied. . . .

Fleeing Reality

From time to time, most people refuse to admit or acknowledge an unpleasant reality. This psychological process of denial makes life look rosier than it is by temporarily pushing away painful feelings or unwanted events. . . . We tuck away painful feelings of anxiety, sadness, loss, and even guilt. As a defense, denial allows us to go about our business acting fairly contented, as if nothing bothers or troubles us beneath the surface. . . .

Eating disorders are significant ways of disavowing psychological pain. Just as people may flee from experiencing physical pain by using sedative drugs or anesthetics, those who misuse food may do so to hold certain feelings and experiences at bay. This distancing maneuver allows the patient to steadfastly forswear certain aspects of her past and present.

> Kelly P. was a lively anorexic woman. At age 22, she had already had her diagnosis for 6 years. In addition to self-starvation, Kelly compulsively exercised to the point of exhaustion. She had several stress fractures of her ankles because of her moderate osteoporosis and intense activity level. She never seemed to stop exercising, although the prescribed treatment for her fractures and her eating disorder was to rest her legs and gain weight.

> Kelly denied her physical pain, her weight loss—even the state of her psychological health. She insisted that she was healthy and plump. Even after her podiatrist placed her ankles in casts, she managed to keep exercising her upper body. To burn up calories, she squeezed her fingers, clenched her hands, waved her arms, and turned her torso from side to side. Yet she already weighed 30% below her designated recovery weight.

What personal saga lay behind a compulsion so severe that it drove Kelly to exhaustion, if not physical compromise and injury, even as she insisted she was fit and energetic? . . .

On the surface, Kelly expressed anger at her mother for being alcoholic. She acknowledged that she had felt abandoned and betrayed whenever her mother left her with her father or a babysitter, only to go off and drink with her friends for what seemed like an eternity. When Kelly's mother returned to their chaotic household, she would emotionally abandon her daughter yet again as she turned her own reserves of emotional energy into screaming barrages at her husband.

In treatment, Kelly gradually began to experience the full force of feelings she had denied for years. Her use of exercise in particular had staved off the rage she felt toward both her parents for what she considered their emotional neglect and abandonment. Exercise also allowed her to avoid the depression and loss associated with this parental deprivation.

Only with difficulty could Kelly begin to see the deep ambivalence she harbored toward both her parents. True, they had been responsible for some realistic disappointments and deprivations in her life. But they had also tried their best to see that she was well-educated and cared for; they had sacrificed so that she could receive psychiatric treatment. She attempted to disavow her ambivalence as she did her need for food, but neither could be suppressed forever. Her emotional struggle surfaced instead in her life-threatening symptoms.

Kelly's actions also indicated that she could endure without her mother's succor; indeed, to have even one "sip" of nurturance might stimulate a desire for more, something her mother might be unable to give even now. By running, bending, shaking, and fasting, Kelly could take care of her own needs and wants that she was convinced no other person could ever satisfy. . . .

By becoming the "thinnest" or "the greatest sufferer," the anorexic patient creates within herself an illusion of power. Her target weight becomes a measurable, achievable goal. She then has the right to feel special, because she has finally "achieved something" grand—but she cannot accept this accomplishment for long.

Because people with eating disorders believe they have sacrificed their own lives for others, they also believe that they deserve to be treated better. They seem to feel entitled to special treatment and understanding. Finally, their illness permits them to turn the tables on those who symbolically or realistically deprived them of their childhood. For once, they hold the power to cause concern and worry; for once, they can demand the care they wish they had received and decide whether to take it or reject it. . . .

Enacting Patterns from the Past

Psychodynamic treatment helps us to examine the important memories and events of the past. Through it, we come to realize how all of us, regardless of our self-understanding, will inadvertently play out the past. We also come to see how our present realities are shaped by the significant qualities of our parents and other loved ones. Yet before treatment, we are rarely consciously aware of this process. In therapy we become more attuned to what those in psychiatric practice call our "identifications and incorporation."

Consider, for example, how often you hear a remark like this: "Little Susie's walk is really just like her father's." These common, everyday comments speak to the degree to which we incorporate aspects of our most intimate relationships, particularly those that are important in our childhood. As we are growing up, we also introject entire situational schemes, repeating them over and over to gain mastery.

A simple illustration of this phenomenon occurs frequently in clinical practice. A mother, never satisfied with the accomplishments of her children, reprimands them repeatedly. She wants them to do exactly what she tells them to do; when they disobey, she withdraws from them even for the slightest infraction. This parent probably learned this disruptive pattern of interaction from her own mother who, inadvertently but somewhat mean-spiritedly, forced her children to submit to her own whims rather than fostering their unique achievements. In any case, the rigid mother experiences herself as being a loving and good mother by enforcing such standards. In actuality, she may be behaving quite aggressively toward her child, unwittingly enacting a pattern that conveys more hate than love.

Children raised in such households often view their parents as cruel, but nonetheless long for their love. They cannot avoid taking in the baneful, erratic qualities they experienced but tend to keep them buried. On a conscious level, they love their parents and want to emulate and please them more than anything. So the child who has identified with the parental drive to control and punish may end up relentlessly punishing herself for any small infraction. Without knowing it, and to avoid being helplessly subjected to her parents' anger, she may also take on some of their haughty, exploitive qualities. Her unconscious intent is to achieve mastery over her environment by doing to others what had been done to her. . . .

One individual, Whitney R., spewed forth recriminations that put even her closest friends on guard. . . . Among her peers, Whitney's hostility had earned her the nickname Junkyard Dog. . . .

Whitney's bulimia was further evidence of her malevolence; with every purge, she became more convinced that she was bad. She called herself a monster. It confirmed to her that her father's early opinions had been right—that is, she was born deviant, ugly, unproductive, and hurtful. His angry tirades resulted in punishments that kept her from forming age-appropriate, positive relationships. When he became angry with her imperfections, he would punish her by grounding her for weeks on end. His tirades led to (among other things) Whitney's deep insecurity, which hindered her from forming good social relationships. For Whitney, the eating disorder and rampant hostility combined to confirm an early object tie with a punishing father. Unconsciously, she was treating herself just as she had experienced her father treating her. She also berated others, as she had experienced her father verbally abusing her, for not living up to an impossible ideal. With her patterns of restricting, bingeing, and purging, Whitney took revenge on herself for not attaining her own very high standards, hoping all the while to gain some control over her body. . . .

Through self-punishment the individual manages to feel quite self-righteous and egotistical, at least temporarily. Her emphasis on perfection holds her to a higher standard than others around her. Yet her hope is to please the object whose love she craves—usually a parent. With the self-sacrifice and aggression she directs toward the self, perhaps she will finally win the love of the sought-after other. . . .

Punishment Means Love

Sometimes a woman acts submissively to win over a person who has been harsh, abusing, or simply critical. Her past leads her to believe that suffering is the only way to connect with others and preserve relationships. She is compliant to win love; otherwise, she feels lonely and abandoned. To stop this pattern requires her to give up an all-important relationship. She is thus caught in a relentless struggle to find love but believes that she can get it only if she submits to control or pain. She might lose the other person if she puts her foot down, becomes assertive, or refuses to obey orders.

To win the person's love, this woman throws all she has into "seducing" the all-important original object, usually her mother. She is terrified of losing this vital tie. She equates eating, nurturing, and being criticized because of their temporal connection so early in life, and so develops an eating disorder as a particularly entrenched and devastating mode of self-punishment. If the eating disorder becomes severe, other people also begin to "punish" the patient by imposing restrictions on her such as structured eating, confronting her about her health, and insisting she enter treatment. Indeed, eating disorder patients unwittingly try to provoke their treaters into establishing a dramatic stance of control, because control is what they are used to. In an equally extreme attempt to get their needs met, they may also try to charm their treaters into a disavowal of the symptoms.

In any case, for some individuals, one hidden meaning behind the eating disorder is that it masks an attempt to bring another person psychologically close by being submissive. Although terrified of doing so, the person with an eating disorder may believe that submission is the only way to obtain love. The eating disorder then becomes a way to render punishment on the self while terrorizing the other person. . . .

Sometimes the individual has experienced so much pain and abuse at the hands of other people that she now has an additional wish for retaliation. In this case, she may need to destroy her treatment, her therapist, or her own important relationships out of a desire to punish her earliest objects whom she perceived as sadistic and hurtful but with whom she now identifies. In a sense, this self-destructive tendency also allows her to feel superior to others and devoid of any need for them.

When a parent is explosive, abusive, prone to addictions, or simply unable to communicate effectively with the child, it can result in a lack of holding and soothing. The child also fails to develop a language that allows her to speak her mind and to participate in mutual exchanges of meaningful verbal connections. She is left to struggle with herself, often without words and caught up in a myriad of feeling states that reinforce her badness and the fact that she deserves pain. If she knows only pain, it will naturally become the only way she can relate to others. . . .

> Melissa S. was a severely anorexic young woman who had defeated many treatments. She allegedly had experienced numerous physical attacks at the hands of her mother. At age four, she was adopted by another family who brutalized her. She saw herself as the victim of others' multiple aggressions against her and bitterly complained the she had been mistreated throughout her life. . . .

> Melissa had a strong need to destroy her treatment because of her identification with the maternal figures who had abused her. She taxed the patience of even the most experienced therapists by making them feel that they had nothing worthwhile to offer her. Their slightest error or imperfection led Melissa to decry that evil had once again been done to her. . . .

Melissa was attempting to turn all those who could do her some good into destructive perpetrators. This reversal helped Melissa hold onto a relationship paradigm she had experienced since her youth—submission, suffering, and destroying the good as a condition for maintaining an important (albeit destructive) relationship. Love came only from punishment! . . .

Using the Intellect Destructively

Clinical work with eating disorder patients confirms that as a group they are among the most extraordinarily bright and talented of people. Sometimes they have been able to accomplish impressively and dramatically in their chosen careers despite struggling with starving, bingeing, or purging. Some may not have been able to achieve to their fullest potential but are still shown to be quite intelligent and capable according to their psychological tests.

Both groups of the achieving and underachieving eating disorder population have this facet in common: given the opportunity, they can use their intellect either constructively or destructively. One potentially harmful way is to use intellectualization to avoid facing one's feelings or life circumstances. . . . Life is lived only "in the mind." The person denies her physical body to focus instead on developing brilliant verbalization skills. Often the words are without much meaning. . . .

Kristen T., age 20, was forced to leave college in her junior year despite her superior academic performance because of her bulimia and very low weight. On the surface, Kristen was committed to her treatment to control her symptoms and explain why she had turned to eating to express her feelings.

One afternoon in group therapy, Kristen poignantly related how her mother had fed her only tiny sandwiches while other members in the family received full-course meals. Her mother's own eating disorder and obsession with appearance had made Kristen feel "like a pig" from an early age. As treatment proceeded and Kristen began to eat differently but normally, she even gained a bit of weight and began struggling with how to integrate what she experienced as a shift in her body image.

During another group therapy session, Kristen became quite tearful as she talked about these changes. Then she began sobbing as she detailed her mother's militaristic control of her childhood diet. In the midst of this incident, Kristen suddenly shut off her tears, looked up and smiled at the group, and bluntly reported that she now understood the reasons for her long-standing anger at her family and the causes of her eating disorder. She then gave a detailed but highly intellectualized formulation of the cause of her difficulties. Beginning by reciting a litany of complaints against her mother who had made her care for an aging grandparent, Kristen concluded by focusing on her father's construction business as an activity that kept him away from home for weeks at a time. She relayed all this information without much feeling at all. . . .

Kristen felt devastated at not having had the kind of unconditional love from her parents she longed for; she was recognized only for her rigorous control of her body through diet, exercise, gymnastics, and academic accomplishments. Small wonder Kristen reverted to intellectualization as a defense: not only was it the only way she knew to cope with highly disturbing feelings, but it also had won her parents' favor and recognition from the time she was small. Human sympathy in Kristen's family was considered a supreme indulgence, so to express sorrow, joy, irritation, or any other feeling was the ultimate "pig out."

A Search for Perfection

As young children, we all look for heroes and heroines, usually in the form of our parents. Later on we transfer our loyalty to other adults with charisma, star quality, or simply the ability to stir deeper admiration within us. . . . But as development proceeds, children gradually become aware of their parents' flaws. . . .

In a sense, idealization gives way to the child's realistic appraisal of the personal fallibility as well as the fallibility of others. . . .

Some eating disorder patients maintain tenacious idealizations in their relationships. These idealizations are best understood as a holdover from earlier development. Thus, along with the eating disorder itself, the person hopes to find perfection in the other. . . .

The cost, of course, is that one can never find the kind of adulation in adult relationships that was longed for in youth. Inevitable disappointment accompanies each failure in empathy and understanding that occurs with human interactions. The life history of many people with eating disorders will include a series of failed relationships. . . . Their tendency to feel disappointed in others occurs because they continue to search for the proverbial Golden Fleece—the mythical perfect human relationship.

Carol U., a 45-year-old stockbroker with severe bulimia, went to pieces in every relationship she established with a man. She usually began a relationship with an older but nonetheless stable suitor, then inevitably found him lacking after a few months. . . .

Carol was, in many ways, a remarkable woman. She could look ravishing in outfits that she had put together from secondhand stores, and she had accumulated impressive wealth during her career. She also had a surprising capacity to attract both men and treaters, all of whom fantasized that they could provide her with the compassion, caring, and cure she needed. This rescuer role played to the conceit and competitive zeal of the treaters, each of whom wanted to "be the best and brightest therapist" to help Carol.

The basis of Carol's search for the perfect other was her own defective sense of self. She needed to idealize others so that her connection with them would make her feel (temporarily) better and more perfect. . . .

Ultimately, her striving for perfection was traced back to her childhood wish for perfect parents and her early belief that her parents wanted her to be flawless. . . .

Carol gradually realized that even her bulimia was related to her search for the Golden Fleece. She had used bingeing like a drug to make her feel whole and soothed, much like an infant in a blissful state of oneness with its mother. This fantasy kept alive the hope that a powerful therapist would fill the parental role and purge Carol of her defects. Meanwhile, she had attempted to rid herself of them by vomiting profusely. Although her eating symptoms were at center stage, they reflected Carol's deep desire to be taken care of by an omnipotent other. . . .

Guilt Feelings About Success

Unconscious guilt feelings lead many career and relationship pathways to a dead end. One might understandably ask what causes these feelings in the first place and why individuals, despite the knowledge that they are not achieving up to their potential, persist in failure. . . .

Many individuals unconsciously believe that success will damage their parents; if they outperform their parents, they may in turn be abandoned by them. Of course, as we reach adulthood we might expect to not continue carrying these childhood fears of loss and abandonment, but sometimes the fears linger anyway.

Furthermore, each individual possesses an internal "parent" who gives permission or forbids certain behaviors based on their accompanying punishment or prize. As a result, we may embark on our life journey with certain internal admonitions or scripts that preclude us from having anything good in our lives. A central belief then surfaces that more is not deserved and, if it is acquired, then it comes at the cost of being abandoned or punished. In wresting defeat from the jaws of victory, such individuals deal with life's hurdles by repeatedly refusing to jump over them. This self-defeating behavior often occurs in the face of significant talent and natural endowments as Katarina's case will demonstrate.

> At the time she began psychotherapy, Katarina V. was 38, single, and had been anorexic for 15 years. Despite her professed desire to marry, she had only been able to engage a series of married men in adulterous affairs. Despite her beauty, charm, and wit that would seem attractive to a wealth of available men, Katarina continued to make destructive choices—although she felt quite ashamed of her past. When one of her lovers decided to divorce his wife and marry her she became terrified at his proposal.

> At this point, Katarina recognized the severity of her eating disorder and her conflict about men. She decided to enter treatment. She expressed a superficial desire to marry and have a family, but when presented with the opportunity, she fled from it. Katarina was in the dark as to what had led her to this self-defeating pattern. Her eating disorder also fueled her relationship difficulties by helping her maintain an aloof stance with men. Whenever she was ill, she could not maintain a romantic involvement, which was one way to protect herself.

> Katarina was also worried about the fate of her elderly mother. As she spoke of her concern that her mother might die at home without her being there, a clue to the cause of Katarina's romantic failures surfaced. To have a man of her own would mean successfully competing with and doing better than her mother. This possibility seemed threatening to Katarina, who loved her mother deeply and did not want to hurt her. . . .

> Her involvement with married men was a compromise. Katarina never attained the status of wife and thus never challenged her mother—in reality or in her own mind. Likewise, her anorexia helped her maintain a less womanly body that precluded more age-appropriate challenges. . . .

All the coping strategies explored in this chapter help to shore up the individual's flagging sense of self. They are heroic attempts to deal with life, albeit less successfully than would be ideal.

Yet psychotherapy can be used to unravel these defense mechanisms and help the individual find new and more adaptive behaviors.

Along the way, the patient benefits by seeing how her therapist deals with life—and his or her own imperfections. It is crucial for patients to remember that their therapists cannot provide either perfect understanding or an immediate cure—nor would doing so be advisable. Instead, life is viewed as a process where growth and changes are desirable. It takes time for the self to grow, but only personal growth will ultimately attenuate the eating disorder.

THE PERFECT BALLET BODY

Kari Gim

In the following selection, writer Kari Gim states that eating disorders are a growing problem in the world of dance. Dancers, Gim says, are under immense pressure to be thin and watch their weight closely. According to Gim, the strong belief of ballet dancers that they must be exceptionally thin to succeed in their profession promotes anorexia and bulimia. In their pursuit for what they consider the perfect ballet body, the author explains, dancers often starve themselves or binge and purge. Gim describes how in the dance world even the healthiest person can fall victim to the obsession with thinness and to an eating disorder.

Jill Cheever had everything going for her. At five feet three inches tall and 105 pounds, the petite blonde had a jubilant personality that infected everyone around her. Once in the dance studio, Cheever's mood would change to a seriousness that reflected her devotion to ballet. She took pride in her training from Marin Ballet and the Oakland Ballet Academy. She and the dance became one; her love for dance was never more ebullient than on the dance floor. No one would have thought she was plagued by a common but rarely mentioned, deadly disease—a disease that can be cured.

Cheever strove to create a name for herself in the performing arts world. She began working at Paramount's Great America in Santa Clara, California, in hopes of attaining a position on one of the dance teams. Her chances, however, diminished as the directors expressed their desire for taller dancers. The rejection failed to tarnish Cheever's dream, and she continued to pursue her goal.

But pressures mounted. Numerous auditions for local theater, dance productions and companies proved unsuccessful. Cheever failed time and time again to catch the eyes of the Great America dance directors. One of Cheever's close friends, Joaquin Guerrero, said he tried to help Cheever restore her self-confidence.

"She became really depressed after not getting anywhere," says Guerrero. "She really wanted to dance for a major ballet company. That was when I noticed a change." Guerrero noticed that Cheever's self-esteem diminished, along with her healthy appetite. Confiding in

Reprinted from Kari Gim, "The Perfect Ballet Body," *Escape Magazine*, Spring 1996, by permission.

Guerrero, Cheever began to think she was too fat. "All she wanted to be was a thin, professional dancer," says Guerrero.

Dangerous Images

Eventually Cheever lost the battle to an increasingly common affliction among ballet dancers and other young women: bulimia. This affliction is characterized by consuming a large amount of food and as a result of guilt, immediately throwing up afterwards. Cheever died in early 1994.

Cheever is one of the more extreme examples of how preconceived images of dancers can highly influence even the healthiest individuals and promote two deadly eating disorders: anorexia nervosa and bulimia.

Anorexia nervosa, from the Latin words meaning "nervous loss of appetite," is characterized by a severe revulsion toward eating that results in extreme thinness and sometimes in death from self-inflicted starvation. Anorexics do not dislike food; rather, they dislike gaining weight, according to clinical psychologist Ellen Schor. She added that victims of anorexia nervosa do not see their bodies as they actually are and feel forced to rigidly control their food intake to avoid "blowing up" to seemingly huge and unattractive sizes.

"When you hear the word 'ballerina,' you immediately picture a skinny girl on stage," says dancer Emily Jones, who asked that her real name not be used. "No one wants to see a fat girl in a tutu."

"Sufferers of these disorders tend to be girls between 13 and 19," says Angela Lee, dietitian at Alta Bates and Highland Hospitals. "They're usually young, healthy girls from fairly wealthy families. They find their physical appearance to be the most important thing in their life. By trying all the diets, diet pills, laxatives and finally starving themselves or going through the binge and purge process, they're striving for what they see as physical perfection. They would literally die to look thin, to look like what they consider 'perfect.'"

Pressure to Be Thin

Dancers face an added pressure to be thin.

Jones, a high school student, dances with the Oakland Ballet. She is a pretty blonde, five feet six inches tall, weighing only a little over 100 pounds. Skinny as a rail, Jones weighed even less just months ago.

In September of 1994, Jones weighed approximately 110 pounds. Immediately following a performance, Jones' mother told her that she could lose about five pounds. "I was pretty shocked at first," says Jones. "I thought I was fine. But I said okay, I'll lose the weight."

Within the next few weeks, Jones lost the five pounds by skipping meals. If she ate too much one day, she'd cut back the next day. She eventually tired of her mother constantly watching her weight. "I planned to get so skinny and sick that my mother would regret telling me to lose weight. I continued losing weight. But my plan backfired and my mother never said anything."

Even though her mother's advice to lose weight did not continue after she lost the first five pounds, Jones says she began to believe she needed to watch her weight. She planned on continuing her dance career once she finished high school and felt she needed to keep a slim figure. "In some ballets, like 'Carmina Burana,' the costumes are very revealing, so no dancer wants to look fat. Then there's partnering. Guys can't lift heavy girls."

An Obsession with Weight

Leaning against the wooden bar at the Oakland Ballet studio, Jones watches a group of younger dancers clad in the traditional school "uniform" of a leotard and tights. Having to pull up the pant legs of her baggy navy-blue nylon pants that look at least two sizes too large for her, she adjusts the ribbons on her pointe shoes. The music of "Don Quixote" stops, ending the younger dancers' pirouettes. Before stepping out on the dance floor, Jones takes off her extra large sweatshirt, but leaves her T-shirt on. "Well, let's see if I'm 'on' today," says Jones.

After successfully attempting numerous double and triple pirouettes on pointe, Jones walks back to the same place at the bar. Out of breath, she smiles at her friends while putting her baggy sweatshirt on. As the next group of dancers try their dance combinations, Jones resumes her quiet contemplation.

Jones says she knows the effects of eating disorders, especially since she knew Cheever. She claims that all dancers watch their weight to a certain extent. "One girl in the company practically lives off of rice cakes and non-fat yogurt, and another girl won't eat any sweets," says Jones. "She won't even have a piece of her own birthday cake."

Friends of Jones still worry about her. "Being out of the ballet scene for a while now has really made me see how obsessive dancers can be about their weight," says Mills College student Jessica Sund.

"I've known Emily for years, and I can't think of a time when she needed to lose weight. She's always been naturally skinny and has that 'ballet body.' I don't think it's flattering to see a skeleton on stage anyway."

"I was afraid when I started seeing all of Emily's bones in her back, really sticking out there," says Caron Aarts, fellow ballet company member. Aarts, wearing long leg warmers, a T-shirt, sweatshirt and chiffon ballet skirt over her black leotard and pink tights, plops down on a bench near a wall of mirrors in the dance studio to take a break and drink her Snapple.

"I saw Jill when she was really skinny and sick, and I thought to myself that Emily could end up like her," says Aarts. "So I constantly talk to Emily, saying that she should eat more. But she's always telling me that she has everything under control."

A Need to Look Perfect

Anorexics and bulimics have much higher standards than the average person when it comes to "looking perfect," says dietician Lee. The victims of both of these eating disorders say they must do well in life and be accepted and well-liked by all. Beneath their facade of self-assuredness, however, they are sensitive to rejection. They tend to set unrealistically high standards and condemn themselves if they fail, according to Schor. Once these victims fall to anorexia or bulimia, it is often difficult for them to conquer the highly emotional and physical battle.

According to Dr. Beth Scroggins, a Bay Area psychiatrist, anorexics and bulimics believe they can control their stress and anxiety when in reality they don't. Then eating disorders take control. In the dance world especially, these victims place higher standards on themselves to look thin and dance well. When these standards aren't met, the victims blame themselves by starving and purging.

"The dancers I know personally are so hard on themselves," says Scroggins. "If they take even a morsel of something 'forbidden' like a candy bar, they immediately regret it. So to punish themselves for this dirty deed, they'll skip meals for hours or even days, or throw it up."

A Growing Problem

Eating disorders associated with the dance world have been increasingly regarded as a problem, according to numerous psychiatrists, medical doctors and dancers. In the book *Off Balance*, American Ballet Theatre principal Martine Van Hamel, one of America's more famous ballerinas, says, "It's necessary to be thin if you're a dancer. But the thin thing is being carried too far. There's thin where you can see your line and dance properly, and then there is too thin."

"So much emphasis is put on being thin that it's neurotic," adds Van Hamel. "It gets to be a sickness, it's crazy."

According to *Off Balance* author Suzanne Gordon, the late ballet choreographer and director George Balanchine promoted the dangerously thin look. "Balanchine has often stated that he likes his dancers super thin because he can see more that way," says Gordon. "Despite its distortions, the Balanchinian aesthetic has become the norm in ballet."

What was the norm for Balanchine has become the norm for many of today's young dancers, including Emily Jones.

"Thin ballerinas may think they're pretty and have perfect 'bony' bodies, and other people may think that too," says Scroggins. "But sooner or later they're going to have to come to terms with these diseases. They may soon figure out the health problem of malnourishment and imbalances of the body's chemistry, or those health risks may affect them first, warning them about their conditions. They're taking a big risk by gambling with their lives."

A Bout with Bulimia

Oakland Ballet dancer Ann Smith, who requested that her real name not be used, agrees. Smith has danced with Oakland Ballet and was a bulimic for several years. Her reason: competition.

"I am very competitive, and to get the lead roles in ballets, I would do practically anything," says Smith. "I gain weight easily, and the easiest thing for me to do to get ahead was purge to lose it." Smith, at five feet two inches tall and now 99 pounds, has gone as low as 85 pounds.

Sitting on the floor of the dance studio in her dance wear, Smith has just finished taking a ballet class during the company's hiatus. She methodically ties the ribbons of her pointe shoes in a neat bow. Taking off her floral chiffon ballet skirt, Smith puts her sweat pants on over her mauve-colored unitard.

"Bulimia is in my past," says Smith. "I was never proud of it. It was my secret all that time. I know I'll never binge and purge again."

According to Smith, Jones looks fine and shows that her weight control hasn't affected her dancing yet. "Dancers fear gaining weight, which may result in not getting to dance any lead roles," says Jones. "Weight can jeopardize a dance career." Smith, however, expresses concern for Jones' condition.

"Emily is technically a strong dancer," says Smith. "But if she continues to keep losing more and more weight, she'll lose that technical edge along with her health. I know because I've gone lower than she has. My energy was zapped, I felt horrible and depressed, and I was close to hospitalization. But I survived with the strong support of my family and friends. Clearly she's got those friends who are there to support her."

Smith said she credits her family and friends for recognizing her problem and helping her through recovery. They warned her about her dangerous condition, and made her see what she was doing to herself and to her loved ones.

Moral support is only one of the recommended treatments for anorexia nervosa and bulimia. The National Association for Anorexia Nervosa and Associated Disorders (ANAD) in Illinois urges family therapy, psychotherapy, hypnosis and other relaxation techniques. Learning as much as possible about both disorders can help confused individuals.

More than half a million victims in this country alone have died from anorexia nervosa or bulimia, and there are thousands of new victims each year, according to author Suzanne Gordon. Some individuals suffer lifelong problems as a result, and if left untreated, these illnesses can be highly destructive to the individual, as well as to the individual's family.

After graduation from high school, Jones plans to pursue a dance career with the Oakland Ballet. "I want to see if I'll like dancing full-time professionally," says Jones. "If I don't like it, I'll definitely go to college. But if I get too fat, I know I'll quit dancing."

THE EATING-DISORDERED MALE ATHLETE

Michael Dobie

Newsday staff writer Michael Dobie has written a number of newspaper articles on eating disorders and athletes. In the following selection, Dobie points out that an increasing number of male athletes suffer from eating disorders and other disordered eating behaviors, including chronic poor nutrition and obsessive exercising. According to Dobie, wrestling is the sport with the highest percentage of males at risk for "disturbed eating behaviors." Men, even more so than women, resist admitting that they have an eating disorder, he asserts. Therefore, he explains, by the time most males are diagnosed as having an eating disorder, their physical health already has been badly impaired or damaged.

A high school baseball star is hospitalized six times, once with his pulse and blood pressure dangerously low.

A college cross country runner is emotionally frazzled, lashing out at friends and teammates, and suffers from anemia and mononucleosis.

A wrestler smiles too quickly and his dry, taut skin cracks. He frequently spits saliva into a can.

These are some of the many faces of disordered eating. But none of these faces belong to women. For years, eating disorders have been considered a women's disease. Now it is becoming clear they afflict men, and particularly, male athletes.

As is the case with women, eating disorders are increasing among men. Of the more than 8 million eating disorder victims in the United States, "about a million and climbing are men," according to the National Association of Anorexia Nervosa and Associated Disorders.

Disordered eating, a more expansive term that includes clinical diagnoses of anorexia nervosa and bulimia nervosa as well as cases of chronic poor nutrition and obsessive exercising, is even more widespread.

Concerns about what male athletes eat and the methods some employ to lose weight have surged in recent weeks with the deaths of three college wrestlers. Each collapsed during vigorous workouts, and

From Michael Dobie, "Losing Weight, Losing Lives," *Newsday*, December 28, 1997. Reprinted with permission; © Newsday, Inc.

all three deaths were attributed to intense attempts to shed weight quickly. As shocking as those events were, however, experts are increasingly concerned about thousands of other male athletes whose eating and weight-loss habits put them at risk for a variety of medical problems.

Those concerns, experts say, are exacerbated by two facts: Estimates of males with eating disorders are rising; and male athletes, as with their female counterparts, are more at risk for disordered eating than their non-athletic peers.

"Originally, eating disorders in all males were under-diagnosed and I think now we're more likely to look for certain kinds of characteristics that might be related to males with eating disorders. Athletics is one of them," said Janet David, a board member of the Center for the Study of Anorexia and Bulimia in Manhattan and a psychologist who specializes in eating disorders. "Male athletes and—especially if you include dancers and models—performers, males who have a high investment in appearance, in weight, are more at risk than other males."

East Northport therapist Cynthia Pizzulli said she is treating three Long Island high school football players who have bulimia, two of whom are captains of their teams.

"I tend to have a lot of males in my practice," said Pizzulli, director of the Renfrew Center of Long Island's Intensive Outpatient Treatment Program for Eating Disorders. Among Pizzulli's male patients have been wrestlers and basketball players, virtually all of whom are of high school or college age.

Many men are reluctant, however, to admit they have a problem.

Rob, a junior and a distance runner on full scholarship at a prominent Midwestern university, endured both anorexia and bulimia. After years of training hard and watching what he ate, Rob began monitoring his diet even more intently as a college freshman. He cut back on his eating so much that besides losing weight he also found himself perpetually tired, extremely irritable and prone to frequent illness. And when he reacted angrily with episodes of binge eating to compensate for slowly starving himself, Rob would force himself to vomit afterward.

After months of fighting the identification, Rob finally admitted he had an eating disorder.

"People who have an eating disorder are perceived maybe as psychological cases or weak-willed or maybe just generally very troubled people. I guess I'm scared of being viewed like that," said Rob, who requested anonymity. "I felt like I had control but I knew that there was something wrong, that I shouldn't be thinking of food all the time, that all that stuff I was doing is not normal."

Statistically and anecdotally, the sports in which male athletes are most at risk for eating disorders include wrestling, gymnastics, crew, cross country and track, football, bodybuilding and horse racing.

"Some sports for men are associated with weight loss, others with the opposite—bulking up," said Arnold Andersen, professor of psychiatry at the University of Iowa College of Medicine.

Disordered eating can have severe health consequences. The most stark examples were the deaths of the three college wrestlers—from Campbell University in North Carolina, University of Wisconsin-La Crosse and University of Michigan—all of which occurred this fall within a six-week period. An eating disorder can cause heart failure due to the loss of minerals and electrolyte imbalance. Other problems include dehydration, kidney failure, erosion of tooth enamel and inflammation of the esophagus from regular vomiting, as well as sensitivity to cold, tiredness, mood swings and lack of concentration.

New research also suggests that men with eating disorders share with female victims a similar risk for premature osteopenia, a weakening of the bones that is a half-step from full-blown osteoporosis. And, like women, a low percentage of body fat appears to play a role in the process.

"Our research, and we have yet to publish the findings so I won't say too much about it, indicates they have the same vulnerability to osteopenia as women," said Andersen, one of the nation's preeminent experts on male eating disorders.

And men with eating disorders find recovery just as difficult and arduous.

"My eating disorder was a wonderful way to just destroy myself," said Gary Grahl, a baseball-football-basketball star in a small Wisconsin town whose battle with anorexia and compulsive exercise led to six hospitalizations. When he was admitted the second time, Grahl said a doctor gave him sobering news.

"He said, 'Right now, your pulse is so low and your blood pressure is so low that if you keep up this routine I won't give you more than a month, and probably less than that, and you'll die,'" Grahl said. "I was so addicted nothing was going to stop me."

Out from the Shadows

One of sports medicine's most confounding problems, eating disorders are little understood by the public. The stigma surrounding the disease, combined with the secrecy and denial practiced by its victims, has long stifled public conversation. Research and education on the topic has increased in recent years, but the majority of that attention has been devoted to women, with the consequence that male eating disorders remain a problem largely cloaked in shadows.

Some researchers have attempted to quantify the issue.

Craig Johnson, a psychologist who runs the eating disorders program at the Laureate Psychiatric Clinic and Hospital in Tulsa, Okla., recently surveyed more than 1,400 college athletes. He found that 38 percent of the males were at risk for what he called "disturbed eating behaviors." Wrestling, at 93.8 percent, had the highest figure for any sport, including women's sports.

Another study of college athletes in 15 sports found that one in seven male athletes satisfied strict diagnostic criteria for bulimia, compared with less than 1 percent of young men in general. (Bulimia, with its cycle of binge-eating and purging, is far more common among men than anorexia. But anorexia still is far more prevalent among male athletes than men in general.)

In a third study, nearly one in five male college athletes in Ohio reported suffering from an eating disorder in the past; one in eight said they currently were suffering from one.

Sport-specific studies have produced similar results. Researchers in Wisconsin, for example, found that 45 percent of the state's high school wrestlers exhibited at least two criteria for bulimia. One study of marathon runners found that a majority were anorexic or showed significant anorexic-like characteristics. And a recent study of lightweight football players at Cornell University in Ithaca found that 42 percent engaged in "dysfunctional eating" while one in 10 showed binge-purge behavior that suggested an eating disorder.

Many horse racing jockeys, who usually begin their careers as teenagers, routinely binge and purge. It's known as "flipping" in the industry. Use of laxatives, diuretics such as Lasix, diet pills, saunas and rubber suits to maintain low body weight also are common. A study of jockeys in Great Britain found that a majority abused laxatives and diuretics. Former or current jockeys who reportedly admitted either flipping or using pills include Laffit Pincay, Jose Santos, George Martens, Randy Romero and Braulio Baeza.

"Everybody does what they have to do," veteran jockey Eddie Maple said. "I've done just about everything there is to do in my 30 years. But the last 15, besides watching what I eat, I've done the rest of it in the sweat room.

"You might go to the laxative and maybe Lasix or some kind of diuretic, but it tends to do too much harm to your muscles and reflexes. I would say there are still some flippers, yes, but I would say the younger guys are relying more on the diet."

The use of Lasix was at the center of a controversy in Illinois, which last year passed legislation making it illegal to supply child athletes with drugs to help them gain or lose weight quickly. The legislation was prompted by a scandal in which the athletic director of a youth football league admitted giving Lasix to players as young as 10 years old to help them stay under maximum weight limits.

The governing body of New York State high school athletics bans the use of any diuretic.

Experts who hoped education would help eliminate incidents such as the one in Illinois are dismayed the trend has not abated. "Eating disorders are still continuing to increase even though there's been a lot of education, especially of people like coaches and dance teachers and teachers in general who work with people of that age," David, the psychologist, said.

The recent spate of publicity has helped, however, in focusing attention on the role of parents in monitoring the eating behaviors of their sons.

"We rely on our teachers to teach our kids but we get involved to make sure they did their homework," said Rich Langsam, whose son Mitchell wrestles and runs track at Massapequa High School where he is a sophomore. "It's the same thing with any sport. We rely on the coaches but we ultimately have to be the last resort for our children to make sure the coaches are pushing our kids in the right direction. I don't want to say I should rely solely on the coach because he knows the sport 1,000 times better than I do. This is my son. I think I should take a role."

Wrestling with Problems

Much of the research on eating disorders among male athletes has focused on wrestling, with its frequent demands on participants to cut large amounts of weight in short periods of time and then quickly add that weight back. The cycle is more extreme for wrestlers who begin the school year playing football, for which they often are expected to bulk up.

One study of Massachusetts high school wrestlers found that 27 percent had binged and 8 percent had vomited. The study of Ohio college athletes determined that two of three wrestlers binged regularly and one in three purged. In a survey of high school wrestling coaches in New York State published earlier this year by West Islip sports nutritionist Karen Sossin and others, 20 percent reported a suspicion that at least one of their wrestlers had an eating disorder.

"It's widespread in that I'd say it exists in almost every school, but I'd say it's not widespread on every team," said Ray Nelson, director of athletic training at Long Island Sports Rehabilitation and a consultant on wrestling policies to the state athletic association. Nelson, a former wrestler at Bellmore JFK High School, comes from a family of wrestlers.

"A lot of wrestlers are sick in season. They have skin problems—a lot of dryness, a lot of cracking, eczema, dry and scaly skin," Nelson said. "A lot of wrestlers don't smile in wrestling season because if they smile rapidly their skin will crack. Their resistance is down because good nutrition is one of the ways we fight off illness."

"Yo-yo dieting" is a term describing the way wrestlers shed weight quickly to reach a certain weight class, then eat and drink heartily after weigh-in to put pounds back on prior to the actual competition several hours later. Nelson said the process is especially dangerous because it puts added stress on the heart. "That yo-yo-ing back and forth is not good. Rapid weight loss dumps a lot of broken-down fat into the bloodstream, which then has to be detoxified," Nelson said. "The systems of the body have to do double-time. . . . If you're asking your body to do twice as much work, it can fail twice as fast."

Often, wrestlers exercise obsessively (for example, running in a hot shower or working out in multiple sweat suits in a heated room) to lose weight quickly. But most of this loss is water weight, which can lead to dehydration. Dehydration can result in electrolyte imbalance, which can lead to heart problems. Other side effects include damage to the heart, kidneys and liver, and a depletion of lean muscle tissue.

Some wrestlers chew gum to curb their appetites, then spit out the saliva in an attempt to keep their weight down. Nelson said wrestlers calculate the weight they lose while sleeping (a practice called "drifting"), count the number of swallows they take at a water fountain and spit into a can they carry around as a match approaches.

"They're definitely practicing pathogenic weight-control behaviors," Hofstra trainer Rick Zappala said. "I've seen everything. I've seen people taking Lasix to get down to weight. I've seen rubber suits. . . . When I see some of the stuff they're doing, it is kind of scary to me. I question it, too."

Zappala recalled working with one wrestler at the 1991 Olympic Festival in Los Angeles. The wrestler cut weight from 154 to 128 pounds in a matter of days and "almost died." After collapsing in the locker room and being hospitalized, he was fed intravenously and resumed normal eating. Within 24 hours, he gained 20 pounds, Zappala said.

The three college wrestlers who died were not as lucky. Two of the victims—Jeff Reese of the University of Michigan and Joe LaRosa of the University of Wisconsin-La Crosse—reportedly were wearing rubber suits when they collapsed. All three, including Campbell University freshman Billy Jack Saylor, were exercising vigorously in an attempt to lose weight to compete in a lower weight class in an upcoming meet.

But reaction to those incidents indicates the difficulty health professionals experience in convincing some in the wrestling community to change their ways. One Long Island wrestling coach with a reputation for caring about his athletes said of the deaths of the collegians, "I guarantee you it was not just from cutting weight. I cut weight my whole life, it never was a problem."

Autopsy reports, however, did blame methods used by the wrestlers to lose weight.

"The problem is coaches don't understand these practices are unhealthy," Penn State physician Margot Putukian said. "They figure, 'I did that. They'll be fine.'"

Zappala said traditional ways of thinking can be altered. "There certainly is a mentality among the wrestling world that, 'Hey, I did it, he can do it,' although that is slowly starting to change," Zappala said.

In 1991, Wisconsin passed regulations barring from competition any high school wrestler whose body fat falls below 7 percent. This year, New York became the fifth state to enact such rules when it instituted guidelines on weight loss and body composition. Officials said the high school governing bodies of 20 other states are considering similar measures.

Tom Howard, athletic director at Farmingdale High School, has had two sons wrestle at St. Anthony's High School. The first, Trevor, cut weight from 141 to 112 pounds as a senior in the early 1990s.

"Trevor has done some crazy things," Howard said. "The day before the match he'd be 4 pounds over, he'd come home and he wouldn't be able to eat or drink. He was a 96 average student; he wouldn't be studying or doing homework. At that time he was nasty, he had an attitude.

"It was almost like I'd seen other kids do it, [so] I knew my son could do it. I knew he would be stronger at the lower weight. Meanwhile, I knew in the back of my mind all he was doing was fighting the scale. The more I watched it, I realized he shouldn't be doing it, but I did it to my own kid. And I'm not doing it to my second kid, so I guess I've learned a little along the way."

Sossin's research on the state's high school wrestling coaches produced mixed results. On the one hand, the research team concluded that the coaches "were ill-prepared to advise on safe and effective methods for weight reduction." On the other hand, Sossin said, "The vast majority are very concerned about nutrition, disapprove of binge eating, understand the importance of exercise, believe their wrestlers need specific nutritional information and believe wrestlers have the potential to develop eating disorders."

Sossin has developed a nutrition education component to complement the new wrestling guidelines being implemented by the state.

"We need to get away from sucking weight," Sossin said. "Maybe people will begin to look at wrestling as a healthy sport. Maybe this will take the stigma away." And maybe, Nelson said, the new programs will help eliminate problems, such as stunted growth, that can afflict wrestlers and other male athletes years after their competition days are over. One study of Harvard students 10 years after graduation, for example, found that eating disorders had dropped in half among the women but had doubled among the men.

"I know a lot of wrestlers have weight problems post-wrestling career because they learn to be in control of their weight. Later in life, when their metabolism starts to slow down, they resort to those odd tactics," Nelson said. "I know guys up to 30 years old who these days are still bulimic, who still throw up after Thanksgiving."

Men and Women

Male athletes who develop eating disorders often share with female victims such traits as being high achievers and obsessive-compulsive perfectionists. But the sexes differ in significant ways as well.

Where many women of average weight "feel" overweight before they begin the kind of dieting that leads to more serious problems, most male victims actually are medically overweight at the onset of an eating disorder.

"They were chubby as children. . . . They were called fat and slobby and all these other things," Pizzulli said. "Usually, they start by dieting and the diet works and someone says, 'You look great.' That's positive reinforcement. Now they've gotten all this attention. One day they slip and have a piece of cake and they say, 'Oh my God, I can't go back to the way I was,' and that's when it happens."

Pizzulli said many male athletes become victims in the wake of an injury. No longer active and fearful of gaining weight while recovering, a male athlete begins to diet. At some point, he loses control.

"It's like getting into a canoe headed for Niagara Falls," Andersen said. "You get into the canoe voluntarily, but by the time you reach the falls you're no longer in control."

Improvement in sports performance is one goal men typically adopt when they begin the kinds of diets that lead to an eating disorder. There are three other possible goals, according to Andersen—a desire not to be teased for being overweight, a desire to avoid weight-related medical diseases experienced by their fathers or a desire to please a gay lover.

The key, Andersen said, is that male athletes, like men in general, view weight loss as a means to an end—getting better in their sport.

"As I got into high school, the competition got tougher. That, I think, was the impetus," Grahl said. "I started to feel the pressure more. All of a sudden, I started to diet. . . . I got into it so much I found it was a way to relieve pressure and tension and it just snowballed."

Most experts agree that once an eating disorder develops, a man might be even more likely to keep it secret than a woman. Pizzulli said that is due partly to the myth that a man with an eating disorder must be gay, an outgrowth of its identification as a women's disease.

What is viewed as an added pejorative frightens many male athletes.

"That's certainly another aspect of why I don't feel like I want to make this public," said Rob, the Midwestern runner. "It would be difficult [with] some of the comments from guys on the team. . . . I think if I got help and people found out, I would never be perceived the same again."

People close to a male victim of an eating disorder often fail to recognize the symptoms, partly because they are not looking for them and partly because men are adept at hiding their behavior. "I didn't want anyone to know," Grahl said. "I was a popular guy and I was good in sports, good grades. I was the last guy people thought would have something like this."

Compounding the problem of identification is the lack of a telltale physical sign for men that corresponds to an interrupted or missing menstrual cycle for women. The absence of such a warning means the eating disorder also goes undetected by a trainer or doctor; often, the disorder is more serious and more deeply entrenched by the time a male athlete seeks help.

Rob, for example, exhibited a number of symptoms of disordered eating during the most serious phase of his illness, when he cut back to 1,200 calories per day while running 70 to 90 miles per week. Even though he dropped below 120 pounds on his 5-foot-9-inch frame, Rob said no one knows he has an eating disorder.

"When I'm having a lot of problems with the eating, emotionally I'm stressed out and grouchy and I'll snap at people easily," Rob said. "Physically, you're tired all the time, you get up and get the big head rushes. A lot of days I feel like I'm just walking to class in a haze, very, very fatigued."

Rob, like many male athletes who are victims, suffered from elements of both anorexia and bulimia.

"When I was cutting down that much, there was a cycle involved," he said. "Eventually, I got so hungry that I would mess up a little bit and eat more than I would want to and you go crazy and lose control and, yeah, I would throw up."

Rob said he used his fingers to induce vomiting and, at times, laxatives to purge. One of Pizzulli's patients takes as many as 45 laxatives a day. Andersen said Rob's pattern of behavior is common for eating-disordered male athletes.

"As they try to push their weight down, their body says, 'Nuts,' and they binge. A binge initially is appetite breaking through," Andersen said. "The purging becomes a way to undo the binge they didn't want in the first place. [Anorexia and bulimia] are really two sides of the same coin, not two separate disorders."

When his behavior was at its most severe, Rob suffered from mononucleosis and anemia, both of which he attributes to his eating disorder. He is not sure what to make of his two stress fractures, but Andersen said an increase in fracture risk seems to be as true for men as it is for women.

For eating-disordered women, amenorrhea—the loss of the menstrual cycle—is an indication of an estrogen deficiency. The lack of estrogen leads to a loss of bone density and, if amenorrhea continues long enough, osteoporosis. This process has become known as the Female Athlete Triad. Andersen said a similar process occurs in male athletes suffering from an eating disorder.

Lower body weight means the bones receive less stimulus from exercise, which weakens bones. Andersen said male eating disorder victims also have higher levels of cortisol, a hormone which leeches calcium from the bones. Men also experience a gradual decrease in the hormone testosterone as they lose weight, which has a negative effect on sexual drive and performance—and bones.

"The analogue to estrogen in women is that low testosterone in men leads to decreased mineralization or bone loss," Andersen said. "The whole body chemistry is changed by the process of starvation."

The testosterone level in a man with an eating disorder can drop to as little as 10 percent to 20 percent of normal—about the same as an average woman, said Andersen, who recommends a bone density test for any "chronically ill eating-disordered" male.

Andersen, who also directs the Eating and Weight Disorders Clinic at Johns Hopkins University, stressed that his research is on-going and that such issues as the rate at which bone loss occurs have yet to be determined.

Search for Understanding

Trying to determine what he might have achieved without his eating disorder is something Rob grapples with every day. In college, his performances have been inconsistent. He has noticed that a bad race tends to follow a week in which he has "struggled" with his eating disorder. Rob still has not sought treatment, nor does he feel he can confide in anyone close to him. He has been comforted only by his own research that has taught him that he is not alone.

"There needs to be an increased knowledge and an increased—I don't want to say acceptability—maybe, awareness. There needs to be more of an awareness of the characteristics of these diseases," Rob said. "And society, or the sporting community, has got to be able to be more understanding.

"For a long time, I thought I had some kind of odd psychological screw-up. But the characteristics that I display are very similar to what a lot of other people are going through and that's sort of comforting."

CHAPTER 3

CARE AND TREATMENT

What to Do to Help

Jean Antonello

Jean Antonello, a specialist on obesity, eating disorders, and co-dependence, is the director of the Naturally Thin Training Center in St. Paul, Minnesota. In the following selection from her book *Breaking Out of Food Jail: How to Free Yourself from Diets and Problem Eating, Once and For All*, Antonello points out that people often need guidance in making decisions about helping a family member or friend with an eating disorder. She offers eight simple guidelines a person who wants to help can follow. According to Antonello, one of the greatest challenges facing individuals who want to help someone with an eating disorder is practicing tough love—telling the person the truth about how the disorder affects them and refusing to be a party to such self-destructive behavior.

The acute/dangerous eating disorder symptoms cannot be ignored because they reflect at least a potentially serious physical threat. And naturally, if you are close to someone and you recognize earlier symptoms of these dangerous disorders, you'll want to intervene sooner. A lot depends on your relationship. . . .

If the eating disturbance is acute/dangerous, the best thing to do is to get professional help. Just getting the person to a doctor for a physical should be the goal in this situation because the physical threat is paramount. Any physician, including the family doctor, will do. You should be referred to a specialist if it's necessary. The only exception to this is a situation where there is a potential for suicide. Then you should try to see a psychiatrist. Find one who specializes in eating disorders, if possible.

It's impossible to tell how serious the sick person's condition is unless she is examined and has lab tests run. Don't project into the future with the person you are trying to help, talking about treatment or therapy. She doesn't need a barrage of "threats" at this point. Just stick with the physical as the goal. When the results are in, the doctor will help her (and you, if you are the parent and she is a minor) decide what the next step should be. If you are not related or this relative is an adult, this may be the end of your helping role.

If the person you love is referred to an eating disorders program and you are a family member, there will probably be some help offered for you. And if you are not a family member, you may be able to participate as a concerned friend. Now it's time for you to get help for yourself and take the focus off the person you have brought.

Guidelines for Coping

Here are some simple rules to follow to help you make decisions about helping the person you care about. It's a good idea to check any idea against this list before deciding on any action you think would be helpful. If your idea conforms to these guidelines, then go ahead. If not, better hold off.

1. Take Good Care of Yourself. Stay in touch with your own needs and limitations. If you have considerable trouble with this, see a counselor yourself. You can probably use the support anyway.

2. Don't Get in Over Your Head. Don't try to be an eating disorders counselor. If you feel that the situation is dangerous, or potentially so, get professional advice. If the person with an eating disturbance won't go for professional help, find out what you should do, and get some support for yourself.

3. Stay Focused on Your Own Life. It's easy to get sucked into the worry world of crazy eating. Don't do it. Do not allow yourself to obsess about the sick person—it will drain you, and it won't help her. Schedule projects or activities you enjoy for your free time if you are unable to keep your mind off the situation. And if you simply can't keep your thoughts in line, see a counselor.

4. Tell the Secret. Besides the professional avenues of support, it's helpful if you tell someone close to you, whom you trust, about the problem. Tell more than one person if you can, so you have options when you need to talk. Do not keep this a secret, no matter how ashamed you may feel about it. You shouldn't be in this alone.

5. Back Off Emotionally from the Sick Person. This doesn't mean abandonment. It means taking a mental step back from a person who can too easily "hook" your emotions in an unhealthy way. It's also called detachment, and it's a method for setting better boundaries between you and the person you care about. Practicing "seeing" the person as a stranger or acquaintance may help you achieve detachment.

6. Back Off Physically, Too. This doesn't mean that you should stop showing affection, it's about respecting the personal space and the physical lines between people. For example, avoid watching the person who worries you choose food or eat. Leave the room if necessary. Make no comments about what you see regarding her choices. Do not go through her personal belongings, looking for "evidence." You may not like what you find, and if you don't find anything you'll still be worried.

7. Limit Sharing Your Concerns. It's senseless to try to hide your worries from a confidant. So after you've brought the subject up once, and found professional help if the person is in danger, limit the times (i.e., once a week) that you share your continued concern. This is called containing your feelings and it is different from suppressing them, only to have them come out later. Talking about them at specific times will help you contain them at others, or deal with them with the support of other people.

The Eighth Guideline—Tough Love

8. Practice "Tough Love." When we love someone it's natural to try to protect them from pain. But the pain that comes from eating problems may be the only motivator for the suffering person to change or get help. So don't interfere with that pain. Don't cover up for her, don't make it easier for her to hide, to believe this is normal, to manage her bizarre lifestyle. This is a big challenge, but it is extremely important.

Molly and Katherine were first cousins sharing a small apartment on a college campus. They got along well and shared most responsibilities of apartment living, including grocery shopping. Their first major crisis happened shortly after Molly realized that something was wrong with Katherine's eating. Until that time each took a turn grocery shopping for the week and the other one made a list of things she wanted. As Katherine's list became more and more "unusual," Molly felt she had to say something.

"I can't buy this stuff for you, Kate, it's all rabbit food. You're thin as a rail. You're not eating enough," Molly declared.

"Just because I eat healthy food and you eat junk doesn't mean the problem is mine," Katherine countered. "You agreed to shop every other week, so you have to. Besides, it's none of your business what I eat. Everybody's thin compared to you."

That last crack really hurt, even though Molly wasn't overweight. Molly's voice was shaking as she responded, "It is my business if you're killing yourself. I think you're getting anorectic and I don't want to see you get sicker. I won't buy your so-called health food. You get your groceries, I'll get mine. I wish you'd get help."

Katherine didn't get help, but Molly stuck to her decision.

Tough love is not about manipulating someone into doing what we want them to. It's about letting another person know that her lifestyle, and its consequences, is what it really is, without artificial softeners. By the way, your refusal to cooperate with someone's self-destructive habits will probably incite anger and possibly rage. These emotions are meant to keep you in line, force you, from fear of the reaction you'll get, to do whatever the dependent person wants: keep quiet, buy supplies, support delusions, play dumb, etc.

HOW TREATING ANOREXIA HAS CHANGED

Steven Levenkron

Steven Levenkron is a practicing psychotherapist and a member of the advisory board of the National Association of Anorexia Nervosa and Associated Disorders. His 1978 novel *The Best Little Girl in the World*, the story of a young woman's struggle with anorexia, brought him recognition as an authority on the disorder. In the following selection, taken from his book *Treating and Overcoming Anorexia Nervosa*, Levenkron describes recent changes in three major areas of treatment: medications, the health care system, and the role of the family. According to Levenkron, progress has been made in treating anorexia with antidepressants. However, he writes, high medical costs and a significant decrease in insurance reimbursement have created a drastic reduction in the amount of long-term medical care that anorexics receive. This situation has resulted in greater emotional and financial stress for families of anorexics because they have to bear more responsibility for care and treatment than in the past, Levenkron concludes.

Twenty years ago *anorexia nervosa* was an esoteric term used by a small group of physicians and therapists who began to see a number of emaciated young girls as patients. Over the years the number of diagnosed anorexic patients has increased at an alarming rate as professionals are better informed in identifying victims of anorexia nervosa. In fact, one out of 250 teenage girls succumbs to the disorder for the sake of losing a few pounds. The disorder will prove fatal to 9% of its victims. Of those lucky enough to undergo treatment, less than half will recover completely.

The medical community and families of anorexics are up against a stubborn enemy. Furthermore, the recent changes in the health care system available to anorexics have resulted in shorter hospital treatment time and have shifted more responsibility for the treatment and care of patients to less-experienced physicians and psychotherapists.

From the Introduction to the Revised Edition of *Treating and Overcoming Anorexia Nervosa*, by Steven Levenkron. Copyright ©1997 by Steven Levenkron. Reprinted by permission of Warner Books.

More of the financial and emotional burden will also fall on families of the victims.

There have been three major areas of change in the treatment of anorexia nervosa since 1983:

- Changes in the health care system
- Introduction of antidepressants in the treatment of anorexia nervosa (AN)
- Financial and emotional impact on families of anorexics

Health Care Practices

First, we must take a closer look at the changes in health care. These changes restrict hospital stay to four weeks, even though in most cases it takes eight to nine weeks of hospital stay to stabilize weight loss in the critical stages of anorexia nervosa and assure that the patient is out of danger. During this stage the hospital provides round-the-clock supervision of eating, drinking, and eliminating processes. To the patient this supervision is an unwanted intrusion, but after a week or so the patient usually begins to adjust to the supportive nature of her caretaking environment.

Treatment is not limited to bringing weight to desirable levels. Correcting unhealthy eating patterns, encouraging healthy elimination practices, and warning the patient about laxative abuse and vomiting are also addressed. A good therapist will also discourage excessive exercise practices. Above and beyond the visible, physical damages remain the invisible issues of trust, dependency, rigidity, intimacy, self-esteem, and identity.

It is during this time she begins to use the hospital staff and other patients as buffers against the grip of her anorexic behavior. In an effective treatment she will share her thoughts with others; she will listen, observe, and feel less alone, thus becoming part of a group therapy process that will *slowly* reduce her sense of emotional isolation. I emphasize that this process takes time, often months, to be effective.

In addition to participating and connecting with other members in her group therapy, an alliance or trust with an individual therapist is necessary. Any "surrender" of disordered eating behavior must be done within a positive patient/therapist climate. Without this positive relationship, the patient merely feels coerced out of her security system (anorexia), and will "cooperate" in order to escape her captors. After hospital discharge she will "get even" with those who coerced her by losing the weight "they" put on her.

Another important component in the slow process of rebuilding the life of the anorexic is the role of the family. Family therapy is an essential element during hospital treatment, to build positive family dynamics and replace the hospital climate of support and trust upon the patient's discharge. The family usually joins its own therapy group, which we call multifamily therapy. In this supportive setting, parents and siblings of the patient talk to others facing the same conflicts and problems.

Every psychiatric hospital is required to develop discharge plans to assure continuity of care. Most hospital staffs are aware of the shortcomings of early discharge, and some provide full-time day programs to assure such continuity. Day programs are expensive, and again insurance payments cover only an additional three-week period.

The key issue to remember, in this age of psychiatric health insurance reimbursement that demands cure in twenty sessions or less, is that people take many years to form their personalities, disordered or not. Time—therapeutic time—is still the great healer. It can't be rushed.

The New Medications

A major improvement in the treatment picture is the use of new medications available to the public through their physicians and psychiatrists, especially those specializing in pharmacology related to psychiatric disorders. One problem: the public has mixed feelings about medications that affect our thoughts and emotions.

Today we are far from understanding how certain changes in brain chemistry affect emotionally disordered behavior. Some researchers and clinicians claim that each disorder is a separate disease entity and requires its own particular medication. Other clinicians see disorders as defense mechanisms developed as an attempted solution to mental pain stemming from a combination of anxiety and depression. Even this second group of clinicians differ on whether the disorder is purely hereditary although chemical in nature, or stems from the individual's life experience both past and present. What are the implications if we use chemicals to correct feelings that are reactions to our lives rather than hereditary chemical imbalances? Are we creating "legalized junkies"? On the other hand, what if we continue to hold on to the concept of mental, emotional, and spiritual purity by refusing to prescribe this medication, thus sentencing many to unhappy and unproductive lives?

Presently there are few if any diagnostic measurement tools to assure us whether a disorder is caused by someone's job, family, upbringing, or a chemical imbalance. The question of whether lives change brain chemistry, or whether brain chemistry is solely hereditary, further complicates the issue.

We come now to the issue of the use of new medications that began with the introduction of Prozac in 1988. Prozac proved so effective that other medications producing similar effects were quickly introduced. . . .

Prescribing the proper medication is an educated guess on the part of the prescribing physician. Family and medical history, and variety and intensity of symptoms are all criteria in making the choice. What makes these new medications preferable to the older antidepressants is the relative absence of dangerous side-effects. Any side-effects are more annoying and uncomfortable than dangerous. This has encouraged physicians to prescribe them more liberally.

There is no test for fluid or tissue analysis to determine which drugs might be most helpful with the least side-effects; the prescriber and patient must simply hope for the best. The end results can range from no effect at all to what appears to be a miraculous change in feelings, thoughts, and behaviors. The duration of these positive effects can be short-term or permanent (as long as one continues to take the medication). None of these medications has been on the market long enough to determine long-term effects to the brain or body. Permanent side-effects that continue after the medication is discontinued have not been noted. The patients who benefit the most from this new group of medications are those who suffer from mild to moderate depression, accompanied by anxiety and obsessiveness.

Unfortunately, the pharmaceutical industry has labelled this group of drugs "antidepressants." There is a stigma attached to one's taking an antidepressant. If we had only referred to them by function, such as "serotonin re-uptake inhibitors," or something akin to vitamins, it would produce less conflict, resistance, and shame among those who benefit from them.

The Changing Role of Family

The third major area of change, and perhaps the one with the most lasting effects on both families and victims of anorexia nervosa, is the role of the family in the recovery process—in financial and emotional terms. . . .

Improving the ability to love and form healthy attachments is vital to recovery. This is not an intellectual process. Insights are useful only when they are consistent and supported with love and appropriate actions.

If you are a parent of more than one child you know that your style of love may work for all but *one* of your children. I have had parents say to me, "I only have one unhealthy child. All the rest are fine." The implication here is that it must be the child's defect that makes her ill. While the parent's usual style of expressing love works for the other child (children), this *one* needs something different. Whether the reason is due to birth order (siblings have a way of affecting each other as they compete for parental approval), chemical or genetic differences, differences in intelligence skills and aptitudes, no two children respond to parental love in exactly the same way. Many parents can take their parenting style so personally that they lose sight of the fact that parental love must meet different emotional needs in each child. They identify their parenting styles as their souls; they see any adjustments as rejection of their core selves. Today in family therapy we talk about family systems; by looking at the family system we shift some of the focus and blame off parents. Parents have to detach their parenting styles from their personal identities to make them more suitable to the needs of the child with psychological disorders or the child who is showing hints and signs that may lead to these disorders.

Parent-child relationships are often loaded with fear, anger, attachment, neediness, impatience, fatigue, love, and hatred. Add divorce and remarriage to the mix and the relationship becomes even more complex. When we examine these elements and their effects on parents and children we can see that rearrangement of the relationship is possible. This can be done, however, only when we as parents give ourselves permission to look at ourselves and our needs and feelings first, so we can see what attitudes we have to change in order to adjust our relationships with our children. It is more difficult to change our behavior if it originates from our own unmet needs or feelings. Such a demand may make us want to blame the child for her problem. That would be less painful than recognizing and letting go of needs and feelings we have lived with all of our lives, or at least since becoming parents.

If you are a parent, you must continue to analyze relationships among all members of your family to understand how one of your children could infer that both nurturing and authoritative (protective) resources aren't available to her. After you have completed this rather exhaustive task (make sure you have support from another person before attempting it), plan how the family system can be changed and she can eventually—sporadically at first—seek support from other members of the family. The change in posture on your part must be consistent and won't even be rewarded for quite a while by your resistant anorexic daughter. . . .

The "Benefits" of Anorexia

A few words to the victims of anorexia themselves: When one suffers from a psychological disorder, overcoming it means understanding its positive points—what you get out of having it. The most common "benefits" achieved by sufferers of anorexia nervosa as related to me over the past twenty-five years are:

- It makes me special.
- It proves I have more willpower to resist food than other girls.
- It's the only way I can say no to people (by refusing to gain weight).
- It's my assertiveness.
- I'm invisible without it.
- It's my friend.
- It gives me a sense of protection.

These are all "benefits" that eventually can be transferred to important people in your life to take the place of the "it." New ways are found to say "no" to others. Other forms of achievement are sought and developed. Ways of feeling visible are found. In general a reliable person or persons can replace all the "benefits" derived from having anorexia nervosa. If you have developed anorexia nervosa, however, you probably don't think much of my suggestions or feel optimistic about finding people whom you will be able to depend upon emotionally. Anorexia nervosa could well be called the "mistrusters' disease." Still, this becomes part of the recovery process: becoming vulnerable toward reliable persons, using them as guides and "mirrors" of your appearance and personality.

You are also, like so many other women, responding to the cultural message about reducing body fat to a minimum. This cultural message has come from women's service magazines, and has spread to Hollywood where we see actress after actress slim herself down to her wrinkled minimum. If the models are waif-thin, and the actresses follow suit, it must certainly seem that it is every girl and woman's obligation to be as slim as possible.

Men do not feel guilty if they fail the "pinch an inch" test, because a similar demand is not placed upon men. Perhaps we should examine our notions of femininity. Thinness has not always been the rule for women, but being alluring has. Alluring adornments on women can be seen on the walls of the pharaohs' tombs, so we know that this isn't a recent fad or cultural trend. Why then have women confused "allure" with being thin, and subsequently pursued this "correct" appearance? Obviously, to attract and sexually arouse men. Unaroused men do not function sexually. One might then view the origins of women's need to be alluring to the propagation of the species. This would mean that at its core femininity has two purposes: to attract men and nurture children. These are extremely politically incorrect statements to make in the late nineties. But if we understand that femininity *begins* with this goal, then we can understand how a commercialized society can transform this instinctive aspect of a girl or woman into the desire to have the "correct" body. . . . These societal changes, and the pressure on women to fit the image, target a very vulnerable segment of society: young girls just coming to grips with their femininity and eager to belong. These societal trends affecting women, family systems, and individual heredity have contributed in launching the onset of this psychological disorder. Regardless of the causes, changes in important relationships and psychotherapy, in some cases combined with medication, can help change the rather discouraging statistics on recovery from this extremely stubborn and tenacious personality-altering illness.

A Greater Understanding

Anorexia nervosa has many "cousins," disorders that have similar personality characteristics: rigidity, perfectionism, inconsolability, detachment, mistrust, and repeated behaviors to reassure one's self and control anxiety. Most prominent among them are Obsessive-Compulsive disorders. There is much debate today about the causes of these illnesses in terms of psychological vs. hereditary/chemical reasons. Both of these illnesses, no doubt, contain elements of each, and for many victims it will mean both medication and psychotherapy. In the past eight years the progress in psychopharmacology—new medications for these illnesses—has taken a great leap forward.

With the increasing interest in treating anorexia nervosa by mental health professionals, doctors, and psychopharmacologists, we have more tools, understanding, and treatments than we have had in the past. We also have a clearer picture of the depth of the psychopathology, or mental illness, behind the victim's refusal to eat enough or to gain weight. We understand that there are issues relating to trust, identity, femininity, dependency, as well as family life, heredity, and cultural influences that must all be addressed with great energy and thoroughness in order to improve the rate of true recovery.

PRIVACY NOT PERMITTED: HOSPITAL DAYS AND NIGHTS

Marya Hornbacher

Freelance editor and writer Marya Hornbacher learned about bulimia and anorexia firsthand. She was bulimic by the time she was nine years old, and a few years later she began suffering from anorexia as well. She remained bulimic and anorexic through years of therapy and five long hospital stays. At the time that she wrote *Wasted: A Memoir of Anorexia and Bulimia*, Hornbacher was in recovery but still struggling with issues of disordered eating patterns. In the following selection, excerpted from *Wasted*, Hornbacher writes in graphic detail about the realities of hospitalization for eating disorders. She describes the hospital surroundings, the nurses, the daily routine, the treatments, the food—and, above all, what runs through the patient's mind as she experiences it all.

The hospitalizations at Methodist Hospital in Minneapolis, Minnesota, have a tendency to blur, one into another, since I was there three times in less than a year. Hospitalizations in general are blurry. The days are the same, precisely the same. Nothing changes. Life melts down to a simple progression of meals. They become a way of life fairly quickly. You used to be a normal girl with a normal life. Now you are a patient, a case, a file full of forms. You may welcome this transition. It may seem inevitable to you. You have been removed from the world. You have been found flawed and wanting. You could have told them this years ago. It is all right, in a way, because there is nothing so sure, so safe, as routine. There is nothing so welcome to the anoretic or bulimic, much as she protests and howls, as a world wherein everything, everything, revolves around food.

And there is nothing so wonderfully conducive to eating disorders as treatment.

The Patient's New World

There are the certainties. You will be given slippers—little socks with rubber treads on the soles—and a paper gown. From the doorway to

Excerpted from chapter 4 of *Wasted: A Memoir of Anorexia and Bulimia*, by Marya Hornbacher. Copyright ©1998 by Marya Hornbacher-Beard. Reprinted by permission of HarperCollins Publishers, Inc.

your room, the room will have a bathroom on the left. You will turn the doorknob, but it will be locked. To your right, built into the wall, a small closet. Three drawers beneath a mirror hung too high to see your butt or even your waist. You will be forced to focus instead on your arms, your shoulder bones, the flesh of your cheeks or throat.

Ahead of you, on the left side of the room, two beds, a curtain shoved back to the wall in between. Apparently you will be sharing the room with another patient. Perhaps the two of you will conspire. On the right side of the room, against the wall, sit two hospital chairs, vinyl-covered, gray metal frames. One of these beds is for you. It will be a hard bed, but you are exhausted. In the hospital you will sleep deeper than you ever have, or ever will again. There will be a little table by your bed with buttons on it. You can turn on the radio, call a nurse, flip the light. None of you ever use the nurse call button, even if you are having a heart attack, because you aren't really sick. To call a nurse would be ostentatious, as if you thought you really warranted worry, as if you were so weak as to want to get well. There will be a window in your room that will look out over rooftops and winding streets. Depending on what time of year you are there, the trees will either be full or bare.

There will be a main room, which will have a television and a long bank of windows looking out over the city on one wall. The rest of the walls will have Plexiglas windows through which you will be watched. The room will have one or two couches, end tables, institutional carpeting covering the concrete floor. You will carry your pillow with you everywhere, in its rough white case. You will sit on it, because the floor will hurt the bones poking out through your ass. Or you will lie on the floor on your belly and move the pillow frequently, from under your rib cage to under your elbows to under your pelvic bones. There will be decks and decks of old cards, board games, news magazines. There will be no fashion magazines, and your friends and family will be warned not to bring them to you, because they are bad for you. They may not bring food or drink. If you are lucky, you will be in a hospital where they are allowed to bring decaffeinated coffee. The coffee is never caffeinated—you might be using caffeine to artificially boost your metabolism, or if you are experienced, your heart rate. In Methodist, not even decaffeinated coffee will be allowed, because you might be using it to boost your weight, knowing as you do that you are retaining fluids.

Suffering the Bodily Functions

There will be nurses, several of them, on rotating shifts. They will be nice, or they will not. There will be bathroom times, usually every two hours on the hour. At those times, a few nurses with heavy, jangling key rings will open the door for you and lean back against the closet door. Everything rests on the nurse: The very nicest of them will let you leave the door open just a crack, a token, and she will talk to you while you pee to keep your mouth too busy to lean down and puke between your legs. Most of them will stand there, door wide, but will avert their eyes and talk to you. They always cross their arms. They act nonchalant. Some of them are not that much older than you. You hope they feel horrible. Some nurses will let you turn on the water while you go, so that the noise of your piddling into the little plastic container—called a "hat"—which measures your fluid output is not quite so thunderous. There are also the awful nurses, who swing the door wide and *watch*. These are the ones who diet. You hear them talking on the nurses' station when they think you aren't listening—idiots, you're *always* listening—about their fat thighs. These are the ones who do terrible, cruel things to their hair, perming it into thin strands of curled straw and dyeing it colors not found in nature. And they stare at you, your pants around your knees, your arm folded over your belly to hide what you can, and when you ask them, "Can I please turn on the water?" they will say not simply no but "Why?" And you will say, "Because this is a little embarrassing." And they will say, "Why?" And you will drop it, sitting there, attempting to will your body into silence.

Taking a dump will become an obsession. Taking a dump will be a topic of conversation, often a topic of terrific bawdy glee among the patients, sitting curled up on the couches, or beached, after meals, laid out on the floor, hands on the belly, groaning, distended, in no small measure of pain. The nurses will eventually get embarrassed and silence you: Let's move on to another subject, they'll say, and silence will seep over the room again. The fact of the matter is that you cannot take a dump. None of you can take a dump. You will beg for laxatives, but they cannot give you laxatives because more than half of you are addicted to them already, and they could kill you. You personally are not addicted to laxatives at that point, and the whole idea of using them for weight loss will seem utterly stupid to you, because it's not *real* weight you lose by shitting all day long. It's just *water* weight, which isn't as *good.* . . . Your bodies are in shock. Your intestines, not used to having food in them, or keeping it, will grip the six meals a day like a vise, tighten on the food, refuse to digest. You will lie in bed at night, picturing each item you've eaten, stuck somewhere, arranged in order of consumption: In your large intestine, Tuesday's meals, compacted but still whole; in your small intestine, Wednesday's and Thursday's, part of Friday's; in your stomach, Saturday's and Sunday's; Monday's meals are stuck in your esophagus and lunging toward the back of your throat. If you go too long without taking a dump—say, six to ten days—they will take you away to another part of the hospital and give you a barium enema. This is a nightmare. Barium is an explosive.

Your day will go like this: You will wake up in the wee hours of the morning with dreams of a boa constrictor wrapping around your arm.

It will be a blood pressure cuff. You will, in hazy tones, ask the nurse how your pressure and pulse read. She may or may not tell you, depending on whether she's a regular nurse on the unit (won't tell) or a sub (will). You will sink back into sleep. In the morning, if you are me, you will wake up very early. This will get you in trouble because they will think you are waking up early to have unmonitored time to yourself, to exercise. You are simply used to waking up early, but you take their suggestion nonetheless and spend these early hours listening to the sheets hiss as your legs move up and down.

When the light turns from dark blue to pale gray, a nurse will come to the door to wake you up. Good morning, she'll say. You'll mumble, Morning. You will stand up too fast because you never, never get it through your thick head that your body is fucked up. You will sway and sometimes fall over, which will put you on watch for the rest of the damn day. You will put on your paper gown, shivering, and get back under the covers to wait until it's your turn.

When it's your turn, a nurse will come to the door and usually hold your elbow as you go down the hall. You will stand on the high-tech scale that was probably constructed for eating-disorder units because the numbers face away from you. When you peer over to look at them, you find your weight reads in kilos. You don't know metric. You are furious. You are in a state of total disarray, as is everyone else on the unit. Most of you have known your weight minute by minute for some time. It has become the center of your life, and this not-knowing simply will not do. You beg to know your weight, because you're new. When you've been there a little longer, you will listen to other new women beg with the same desperation, and you will exchange little knowing glances with the others in the hall. They never tell you. Your life comes apart at the seams.

You live, all of you, in a state of constant, crazed anxiety. You know you're going to gain weight. There's really no way to get around it. You can play all sorts of little games, and you will still gain weight. There is no way to describe the tiny, constant implosions of your chest when this thought hits you, as it does, often, day in, day out.

You take a shower in a stall with no curtain. You have to sit down on the little stool in the shower. You argue with the nurse about this. "Why?" you ask. Most of the nurses will turn away in the chair where they keep watch, but not all. You will learn quickly which nurses you hate, which ones you do not hate. The ones you hate will watch. Because you are a little bitch, you will ask the one you hate most, "What, are you jealous?" She will attempt to shake her head in scorn.

But she is jealous. Most of them are not. Most of them think you're pitiful. But a very few have, shall we say, eating issues of their own. You have a trump card.

Your forbidden things will be kept in a little plastic cubby in the nurses' station: Razors, matches, cigarettes. You will be allowed, upon request, to shave your legs. Most of you will shave your legs every day. You will also agonize daily about what you will wear, and you'll apply your makeup perfectly, and curl and tease your hair, as if you had somewhere to go, as if you will not spend your day and the next and the next on the eighth floor of a hospital, with no one to see you but the nurses and the other fuck-ups in the cage. Almost all of you have been spending at least an hour daily refining your appearance since puberty. It is part of your routine, and your routine must be maintained, if only in name.

You will sit in the main room playing solitaire on the floor. You like mornings, because you feel peaceful then. You look forward to your day. Every day, the routine is as such: Breakfast, morning check-in, physical therapy, snack, morning class, lunch, occupational therapy, snack, free time, dinner, visiting hours, snack, evening check-in, bed.

It's like being at camp.

All About Food

You will not realize until you get to treatment just how deep and abiding your obsessive love of food really is. It's not the way most people like food—the feeling of fullness, of communion with friends and family. Food *qua* [as] lover. I remember the day I met Jane as she sat on a couch, doing something to an apple with her mouth that was positively erotic. She was still pretty sick. I asked: What are you doing to that apple? She looked up at me, startled, her tongue on the wet, white flesh. She laughed and said, "I'm making love to it." It was funny, but true. With both anorexia and bulimia, food becomes the object of your desire. You either prefer the desperate hunger of unfed passion, or the battering cycle of food moving in and out and in and out of your body in a rhythm that you never want to end.

Treatment, that first time, turned out to be divine. I had it easy. I was classified as bulimic, so I did not have to gain too much weight. I got to avoid the weird agony some of the other women were going through, though I would later experience the frenzied panic at weight gain upon my frequent returns. Treatment, that time, turned out to be a grand buffet. They feed you normal food, and lots of it. In earlier years, eating-disorder facilities were big on force-feeding and providing massive quantities of high-calorie food, but they soon figured out that this treatment gave way to almost immediate relapse. Now they give you a nutritionist who attempts to convince you that food is simply a necessary thing, neither Christ nor Antichrist. After the first week, when I flat-out refused to eat anything—it was more a statement than an actual fear of food—I went through the motions that we all went through, bitching and moaning about how awful it was to have to eat, balking at the slightest drop of grease on our poached fish, taking as long as we possibly could to finish our food. The fact was, I was in seventh heaven. My life revolved around meals. Never believe an eating-disordered person who says she hates food. It's a lie. Denied food, your body and brain will begin to obsess about it. It's the survival instinct, a constant reminder to eat, one that you try harder and harder to ignore, though you never can. Instead of eating, you simply *think* about food all the time. You dream about it, you stare at it, but you do not eat it. When you get to the hospital, you have to eat, and as truly terrifying as it is, it is also welcome. Food is the sun and the moon and the stars, the center of gravity, the love of your life. Being forced to eat is the most welcome punishment there is.

In the little eating room, a nauseating late-1980s aesthetic will prevail. Heavy on the mauve. There will be a schoolroom clock on the wall, round glass face glinting with the ugly light of those long, humming fluorescent bulbs. You will stand in the doorway for a minute, looking for your tray. It will have your menu beside it. You will spot it, like spotting the face of a lover in a crowd, move toward it, feign disgust, pull your chair back, sit down. At first, you will honest-to-god be mortified, and really not hungry. Your stomach is shrunken, you are very simply afraid of food, and you will cry in despair. But as the body begins to come alive again, you begin to feel hunger, a racking sort of hunger, and you will damn near cry for joy.

Your menu: you have been given a chart, which tells you how many calories you have to eat per day. It breaks that number down into categories: Proteins, breads, milks, vegetables, fruits, desserts, "satieties" (fats). These numbers dance like sugarplums in your head. The obsessive-compulsivity that you used to channel into hyperactive management of time and work is rerouted to a place where it can do some *real* good, and it twitches in your face like a tic when you sit down, each day, with your chart and your menu. You spend hours poring over it, trying out every possible combination of items that might fulfill your quotas. You love the neat X in the box, the tidy circle around optional items, butter and jam, French or ranch. You will look forward to every meal, every snack, with a completely ridiculous level of excitement. All of you will pretend to dread them. All of you are full of shit.

Big Sister Is Watching

This time around, it will be summer. At meals and snacks, someone will turn on the radio, which sits on the counter running along one wall, under the cupboards where they keep the Ensure. You will remember the Ensure, a nutritional liquid that you will get when you do not finish your food within the allotted time: half an hour for meals, fifteen minutes for snacks. As soon as you walk into the room, a nurse will look up at the clock and write down a time on the white dry-erase board on the wall. A nurse will sit down at the head of the table to watch you. She will not eat. She will not read a magazine. She will simply watch you. If she is young, she will join in the conversation, if there is one. Usually there won't be because you are all peering suspiciously at your food. If she is old, she will not talk. When the conversation inevitably turns to food, weight, exercise, she will speak. That's a nonissue, she'll say. You will find this incredibly ironic.

She will scrutinize your eating habits. If you are scraping the tines of your fork against your teeth, even silently, if you curl your lip back from the food in an involuntary sneer, if you are pushing your food around on your plate, or eating things in a particular order, day after day, as I did—liquids first, followed by vegetables, starch, fruit, entrée, and dessert if you do any of these things, the nurse will pipe up: Marya, that's a behavior. When you are new, you'll ask, A *behavior?* You will sit there, trying to keep your lip as far from the food as possible without being obvious, thinking of all the connotations of a *behavior.*

Or if you commit a cardinal sin—spitting food daintily into your napkin, folding it expertly under the table, casually slipping the pats of mandatory butter into your pocket, hiding the last bites of food under your tongue (hiding it in your cheek never works, your cheeks are sunken and stretched)—you will find yourself in serious shit. If you do not finish your meal on time, you will be kept after. You will sit, with one or two other girls, while the nurse calculates the number of calories left on your plate. How are you figuring this? you cry. How do you know how much Ensure to give me? That's too much! That's bullshit! Watch your language, Marya, she warns as she pours the white liquid into a little plastic cup with measuring marks along the side. You will be given ten minutes to finish the Ensure. I'd speed it up, she'll advise, watching you sip as slowly as you can. You're making a choice, she'll say. This is supposed to be empowering. If you do not finish, you will be tube-fed.

You will remember the silence, the ding of tin fork to plate. You will remember the radio, KDWB bouncing along. Everyone will come to know every song on the playlist backward and forward. You will remember a table of women, intently staring at their food, glancing at one another's plates, unconsciously mouthing the words to the songs between slow bites.

RECOVERY HURTS

Jane R. Kaplan

Jane R. Kaplan is a psychotherapist and writer who teaches therapists and other health professionals about the treatment of eating disorders. Kaplan refers to her special expertise in helping
people with eating problems as Optimal Eating. According to
Kaplan, it takes a large amount of time, energy, and determina-
tion to recover from an eating disorder. A person with an eating
disorder who undergoes psychotherapy, she explains, generally
experiences five stages of recovery. Recovery, Kaplan writes, is
"dreary" and without daily rewards. In particular, she notes, the
second stage of recovery, which brings increased awareness of
the eating disorder, is extremely difficult. However, according to
Kaplan, those who make it through all five stages of recovery are
transformed; they become able to voice their feelings and anxieties instead of using food as a substitute.

"I want to recover from this eating disorder more than anything! I'd
do anything to not be bulimic any more." Yes, recovery is the goal. It
spells freedom from obsession with food, getting yourself back, getting your life back and having the energy to concentrate on people
and things without the haze of body and self-hate clouding the way.
There are so many benefits to you, from saving money on binge foods
and doctor bills to feeling you can go out to a restaurant with friends
and not worry. Recovery is great.

However, recovering from an eating disorder using psychotherapy
is also nothing if not a pain in the neck. It takes time, money, perse-
verance, humor, trust, hope, support, dogged persistence and some
really good treatment. Understanding the stages of recovery can make
the process more bearable and maybe even interesting.

Of course, there are a lot of theories about recovery and no one
person could ever fit any theory to a "T" nor could any theory fit all
people.

Optimal Eating's stages of recovery presented here are based on my
twenty years of experience helping people recover from eating disorders.

From Jane R. Kaplan, "Why Does Getting Better Feel So Bad? Optimal Eating's Five
Stages of Recovery," Optimal Eating website, http://www.healthyeating.com/
article.html (2/23/98). Reprinted with permission from Optimal Eating.

Please note that many people who recover from eating disorders are in "team treatment" which includes medical management by a physician, nutrition management, psychiatric management for medication evaluation, and psychotherapy. This team treatment is, in fact, the state-of-the-art treatment for many people with severe eating disorders. In this article, I am addressing the process of recovery as seen from my point of view as a psychotherapist. I am not addressing the many important aspects of recovery which have to do with medical management and with nutritional management. Also, I'm not discussing other forms of healing which are used in addition to psychotherapy, such as Overeaters Anonymous. Yet I believe that the other forms of treatment and help listed above can be an integral part of the healing process. . . .

When I discuss these stages with my patients, most agree that it fits a part of their experience of recovery, and it also explains why recovery is such a pain in the neck. . . .

Stage One: Pre-Recovery

Compulsive eating, bingeing, purging, and starving are "acting out" behaviors. You are using actions, not words, to express yourself. Conflict or inner need is not dealt with directly, but is shrouded in behaviors like binge eating. The good thing about acting out is that the inner pain is reduced. The troublesome emotions, thoughts, and feelings all get channeled into the actions. Between, for instance, bingeing and purging on the one hand, and self-hate on the other, all kinds of other feelings, even excitement and happiness, are pushed far away. Well, not entirely. Feelings really don't let themselves be pushed that far away . . . they have a funny way of coming back. But, in some ways, the pre-recovery stage has the (negative) benefit of keeping troublesome feelings and thoughts away.

Of course, when you overeat or restrict food to cope with problems, avoid painful feelings or maintain a sense of control, there is a real sense of frustration and shame about it. At the same time, since the acting-out behavior is strongly in place, it functions to push away problems, including the anxiety and shame about being eating disordered.

People seek help for a variety of reasons. Shame may become overpoweringly strong and the eating disordered person can no longer bear it. Another motivation is the passage of time. When the "I can beat this myself, I don't need help" attitude has lasted several years without results, help might be sought. Time can be an influence in another way, too. Perhaps it was somewhat acceptable to be a binge eater at 22, for it seemed that binge eating would surely be outgrown by 25. At 28, however, it is quite another story and the eating disordered person becomes clear about not wanting to take this problem into her 30s, into her family life, into parenthood.

Another factor is support. A supportive primary relationship or circle of friends may make it possible to consider getting help. Growth of self-esteem in other areas also plays a role. For instance, as esteem grows in the workplace or in a parenting role, there is a sense that "I can tackle my anorexia too" and treatment is sought. Economics, too, are a part of the picture. A new job or new health insurance plan makes treatment more feasible and provides an impetus. Usually, many factors converge to propel a person out of pre-recovery and into psychotherapy.

People in Stage Two of recovery often look back with nostalgia on their old acting-out days. Ignorance is not bliss, but at least it's better than Stage Two Recovery. Anything is better than Stage Two Recovery.

Stage Two—The End of Many Illusions

Now we're talking pain in the neck. In Stage Two, you engage in a therapeutic relationship and, of course, try hard to use food less. You try to limit your acting out as you should. However, this often hurts a lot.

Remember, the acting out was used to manage troublesome feelings, and, indeed, all kinds of thoughts and feelings. Now you're not engaging in the eating disordered behaviors, or not engaging as much, and all those feelings are there, with no place to go!

Even if you are engaging in eating disordered behaviors, those behaviors begin to function less well for you. They don't numb your feelings and thoughts as well as they used to. You become more aware of your feelings and thoughts and can't push them away . . . but you don't yet know what to do with them. Ouchhhh!

Stage Two is characterized by:

1. The struggle to not act out.
2. A heightened awareness of your eating disorder, which can mean greater awareness of shame about it.
3. A heightened awareness of your feelings, including feelings of low self-esteem, guilt about having an eating disorder, anger and a range of upsetting feelings.
4. A desire to not use food to manage these feelings.
5. Very underdeveloped skills for managing these feelings without food.
6. Increased anxiety that all this is going on.
7. A desire to not use food to deal with the anxiety.

In addition there is:

1. An adjustment to the idea of therapy—"who is this counselor person and why is she/he helping me . . . I don't deserve help."
2. An adjustment to the idea that one cannot do it all oneself, but needs help.
3. Annoyance and relief that a professional counselor is getting to know about your eating problems, which may have been largely secret.

And worst of all: Slow, maddeningly, painfully slow progress in developing other skills, in building self-esteem, in learning how to not act out, in learning other, healthier modes of self-expression. You can see that Stage Two is no fun. It is, in my opinion and that of many of my patients, the most difficult stage. It's also the stage where some people drop out of treatment, and it's not hard to see why. Stage One's acting out is much less painful in the short term. Of course, remaining eating disordered is much more painful in the long term.

Stage Three: The Payoffs Begin to Arrive

Throughout Stage Two you may have asked yourself, "Why am I doing this?" The only answer that comes back is "because I don't want to be eating disordered for the rest of my life." But, on a day-to-day basis, there were no payoffs—no fun or pleasing things about the recovery. It is dreary.

Stage Three is a lot more fun. Slowly and painstakingly the work on not acting out begins to reap benefits. It's easier to control the eating and/or restricting behaviors. You learn new behaviors, and some of them actually work to make life easier. For instance, a bulimic may binge and purge less. She may find her new yoga class really is soothing. She may find she is less self-critical and there is a better relationship to self. Self-esteem is noticeably, if only a little bit, better. Understanding of the factors which led to the eating disorder in the first place progresses. This understanding helps further reduce self-hate and therefore enhances self-esteem.

Relationships to others become noticeably, if only another little bit, better. There are things to point to, things to feel proud of. Change doesn't feel bad all the time. It feels bad only half the time. The other half of the time, there is a tiny bit of satisfaction, of progress, of relief, "So this is what recovery feels like. It's not so bad. I like feeling a bit more comfortable with others. I like this strange lack of severe self-criticism."

Therapy sessions are not as torturous. In fact, things can feel so good that you can declare, "Therapy's over!" It's not, but there is a light in the end of the tunnel. Therapy won't last forever. As Stage Three progresses, you consolidate these gains. It's easier to not use food to handle problems or feelings. It takes more to trigger a binge or restriction. Regressions or slips are, of course, part of the picture. They are lessons and they show where more work has to be done. Forgiving yourself for slips becomes a tiny bit easier than in Stage Two. There is less all-or-nothing thinking. You learn that a slip is not the end of the world.

Stage Three is characterized by:
1. Relief to be out of Stage Two.
2. Awareness of a diminishment of self-criticism.
3. Feeling very strange about this diminishment.
4. Pride in having more control of food.
5. Feeling good about not thinking in extremes.

6. Becoming interested in the origins of the problem.
7. Feeling discouraged because you are not all better.
8. Nostalgia for Stage One, where acting out still helped.

Stage Four: Who Am I?

Throughout Stage Three, identity has been slipping away.

"If I am not bulimic, then who am I?" You go from a primary identity of "I'm the person who isn't nice, isn't deserving and has an eating disorder" to a "transitional identity" of, "I am all those unpleasant things, but I am also a therapy patient. I am working on my recovery." This transitional identity holds for a while until a more major identity is formed. Feelings of low self-esteem are replaced by feelings that you might just be more worthwhile than you had thought.

However, like the roadrunner T.V. cartoon after the roadrunner gets run over, recovering people can feel flat as a pancake. It takes them a while to "puff up" again. Unlike the roadrunner who just puffs up as if by magic, you must work on cultivating other aspects of yourself which have been squished by the eating disorder.

The inner dialogue begins, "Do I like music, art, sports, books . . . what do I like? I don't know if I know." Sometimes, old interests are rekindled. Sometimes old interests won't rekindle and new interests must be developed. Activities are tried to see what clicks.

Relationships continue to improve. For those who are dating, healthier partners are chosen. Relationships become based less on caretaking and more on mutuality.

Recovery doesn't seem so bad after all. Food recovery continues. Your eating disordered behavior is less frequent now. "I tried to binge but I couldn't" replaces Stage One and Two's "I can't stop myself." You have gathered enough strength so that, to paraphrase Dr. Arnold Andersen's words (Dr. Andersen is a well respected researcher in eating disorders and an expert on men and eating disorders), you have outgrown your eating disorder.

Recovery feels different from what you imagined. Like puberty, you can read about it, but the reality of going through it is different. What was imagined in the acting-out time is sometimes the wish to recover from the food problem but have everything else stay the same. It's like putting in an order, "I'll take no bulimia, but give me the same low self- and body-esteem and the same feelings of not deserving support or relaxation." The reality of change and recovery become clear. "I am different, I am stronger, and yet I am still me."

The transition can seem unexplainable in words. It can feel like "it just happened." At times recovered people express thoughts such as, "I don't know how I did it. I can't tell you how it happened. I just got better." Really each person is doing a lot; gaining strength and skill along many important dimensions, replacing old behaviors with new ones, replacing unhealthy control of food with healthier forms of self-control, gaining the ability to tolerate conflict, uncertainty, feelings, thoughts, relationships and change. The recovery is part of a process of tremendous personal growth.

As recovery proceeds, those people in group therapy think of ending group therapy. After all, why be in a bulimia group if you are not bulimic? Goodbyes to trusted group members can be sad, but the pride of recovery and seeing oneself as an inspiration to other group members is satisfying. Those in individual therapy think of ending treatment and some do. Others continue to work on improving and strengthening relationships to self and others still more.

It is not uncommon for an unattached person to enter a period of dating, or for a new, positive, intimate relationship to form. As the eating disorder continues to wane, how to form and maintain healthy relationships becomes the goal of recovery and therapy. In fact, this time of work on health in relationships is Stage Five.

Stage Five: How Do I Deal with People?

There is little or no eating disorder now, but there are many questions. Now you are contemplating dating, or being in a long-term relationship as a person without an eating disorder. Relationships feel very different at this stage. The eating and/or restriction used to function as a back-up plan. If something went wrong in a relationship and you experienced hurt feelings or guilt, there was always the eating disorder to help you escape. Now, conflicts in relationships are clearer. Even if you have dated and have had long-term relationships, you may now feel exposed, inexperienced, and insecure.

This stage could be named "friendships and dating therapy" since so much of the emphasis is on how to form and maintain healthy relationships. Many people experience a new level of clingyness to their therapist. Frightened, they ask, "How do I deal with those human beings out there? " Sessions can be filled with questions about what's normal and reasonable in relationships. Those who have suffered childhood or other sexual abuse learn and integrate new rules for relating.

Slowly, skills are honed. Assertion is often one of the most important. Another is to become more self-focused in your thinking—to think in terms of strategies which take you closer to your goals in regard to a relationship. Many people with eating disorders think in terms of meeting others' goals and sometimes can't define their own goals at all. For instance, a recovering person may be dating and have the goal of forming a committed relationship, but may be unable to focus on her goal. Rather, she may focus on her partner's goal, which could be to further his career or improve his self-expression.

As Stage Five continues, insight develops into why certain relationships haven't worked out. Patterns are explored and changes are made. Though anxiety-provoking at first, Stage Five often ends with a lot of satisfaction as patterns unfold and changes are made. As you learn healthy ways for you to be in a relationship, you realize you can apply them to many relationships, from work to your personal life. "People are strange, but I think I'm getting the knack of relating to them," is a feeling typical at the end of Stage Five.

It is not uncommon in Stage Five for people who are dating to meet more equal and adequate partners. Some cannot believe that they have met and are dating such nice people. They didn't think it would ever be their fate. The "pinch me" feeling prevails. Over time, the unbelievable becomes believed. Those in committed relationships often work hard to change the status quo and shape the relationship into more of what they need. It is an especially joyous time when Stage Five ends in the fulfillment of a much-desired goal.

As you progress through the five stages, you are completing a major piece of work. You have every reason to feel proud of a job well done. You are yourself, but you have been transformed. You have developed a voice to express and take care of yourself. You no longer use food to speak for you.

Finding Qualified Practitioners

To engage in psychotherapy for the treatment of eating disorders, it is important to locate a well-qualified mental health practitioner. . . .

It is best to look for a licensed and experienced practitioner, someone who either specializes in helping those with eating disorders or who has worked extensively in this field. Local eating disorders treatment programs as well as local hospital and physicians' offices can often provide names. Your local psychological association, social work, counselors or psychiatric association can help provide referrals.

After calling and, perhaps, meeting a few different practitioners, you make a decision about who is best for you. You are looking for someone with whom you feel comfortable and whom you feel understands you and can help you. During the process of therapy, feel free to talk with your practitioner about your feelings and your progress. You are in therapy to work hard to get better. As you go through treatment, there should be signs of progress which you recognize. If there aren't, bring this up directly with your practitioner. Therapy should, among other things, be a dialogue in which your concerns are addressed in a straightforward and productive way.

WHAT HAPPENS WHEN INSURANCE COMPANIES WILL NOT PAY

Cynthia Fox

In the following selection, writer Cynthia Fox describes how the development of health maintenance organizations (HMOs) have influenced the treatment of eating disorders in the late 1980s and the 1990s. She explains that HMOs—for-profit groups that contract with medical facilities, physicians, employers and individuals to provide medical care—focus on cutting medical costs by controlling the type and amount of health care covered for specific disorders. According to Fox, most HMOs and other insurance companies will no longer pay for sufficient treatment for anorexia even though it has a higher mortality rate than any other mental illness. As a result, explains Fox, many anorexics are being forced to discontinue treatment long before they should. In addition, she notes, more than three-quarters of the top eating disorders clinics have closed because of insurance problems, leaving patients with no place to go.

More Americans die of anorexia than any other mental illness. Yet insurance companies are refusing to pay for necessary care. Doctors have a word for this—torture.

Crouching by a highway in 100° Kansas heat, Jayme Porter shivers in a cold that doesn't exist. She's nauseated, but because she's starving, she's too weak to throw up; she's dizzy, but because there's no fat padding her bones, it's too painful for her to sit on the ground. Sundae-colored cows graze alongside oil derricks, and excess-crop fires simmer on the horizon. But Jayme perches at the edge of this world of plenty, looking as if she's barely there, for her body is cannibalizing itself.

An hour later, Jayme, 20, meets the Wichita hospital doctors she has traveled three hours from her home in Oklahoma to see. They make a surprising discovery. Since Wichita's eating disorders program reluctantly released her two months earlier—at a dangerous 40 pounds underweight—because her insurance policy wouldn't cover the stay, no one has been providing her medical care, even on an outpatient basis. She weighs 81 pounds. She has trouble finding a job; some employers think she has AIDS. She has a handicapped-parking permit (her ravaged heart makes it difficult to walk), yet the parking space she uses most is at the gym where she works out obsessively. She's a severe anorexic, and the sister of a severe anorexic, yet because her insurance policy doesn't begin to meet her needs, she has been drifting from therapist to therapist, each assuming the others had been doing basic medical tests. None had.

Jayme is in for another surprise: Dr. Tamara Pryor, who has been treating her as an outpatient for one hour every two weeks, announces that even this may soon end. The Wichita program is about to go under for the second time in two years because so many patients lack adequate insurance. All studies indicate that the sicker Jayme gets, the more difficult it will be to cure her. Yet the sicker she's gotten, the less treatment she's received—and now she's faced with none. It's a situation her doctors understand, for in the past few years a bizarre paradox has emerged. Anorexia is the mental illness with the highest mortality rate—15 percent of the more than one million Americans who have it will die—yet it receives the least sufficient insurance reimbursement. But Jayme doesn't understand. "I'll still be able to see Dr. Pryor, right?" she asks. No one answers.

Torture Rather than Treatment

Managed care—the cost-cutting approach adopted by nearly all insurers—has gutted the eating disorders field in the past 10 years. In the mid-1980s severe anorexics would stay two to seven months in hospitals until they reached ideal body weight. But stays for severe cases now range from two days to two weeks, with some insurers imposing a $10,000 lifetime cap, enough to cover about 10 inpatient days, or, as in Jayme's case, a $30,000 lifetime limit. All this despite studies indicating that most patients released underweight need rehospitalization. Doctors now tell 70-pound patients they must be sicker before they can be helped, the equivalent of "sending patients with strep throat away, saying they can't be treated until it causes kidney failure," says Dr. Walter Kaye, head of the University of Pittsburgh's eating disorders program. Adds Stanford's Dr. Regina Casper: "We actually convert people into chronic patients."

Some doctors spend more than 10 hours a week arguing with insurers. "They wear you down with untrained reviewers, then make you go through three or four levels of appeals," says Dr. Arnold Andersen, who runs an eating disorders clinic at the University of Iowa. "It's like trying to stop the ocean." Insurers generally won't reveal their rejection criteria, never see patients and make all judgments by phone. As a result, Andersen says, "every third case that needs hospitalization is not allowed in now." Dr. Elke Eckert, head of the University of Minnesota program, says that 40 percent of her patients are discharged before they should be. Adds Dr. Dean Krahn, who headed programs at the University of Michigan and the University of Wisconsin that folded because of insurance problems: "Patients gain five pounds and are discharged now. You get their anxiety up as high as it can be because they've gained weight, but you haven't had time to do anything that will help them accept it. It's torture rather than treatment." The prediction of many doctors: The 15 percent death rate will rise.

In the last few months of 1997 the problem has become even more urgent, as doctors have realized there are only a few top-notch programs left. If you have a severe eating disorder now, you may find not only that insurance won't pay for your care, you may find, as Jayme Porter did, that you have nowhere to go.

A Need for Supervision

Back home in Stillwater, the day after she discovered the Wichita program might close, Jayme eats an apple for breakfast instead of the juice, yogurt, meat, cereal, milk and two fruits prescribed. She heads for Oklahoma State University (OSU) for the lab tests that should have been done months ago. Then she sets out on her daily walk wearing a 20-pound knapsack that "helps me work out."

No one who spends a day with Jayme can wonder for long why severe anorexics need supervision. After her walk she returns to her trailer—the one her parents started out in and is now hers—parked outside the campus. She pours diet Mountain Dew into a 49-ounce tumbler, explaining it has more caffeine than other sodas and gives her a buzz. She slips on a neon-orange minidress ("I get a rush seeing my skeleton") and checks, as she does every day, to make sure her forearm fits in a circle formed by her thumb and finger. Then she spends an hour in a ritual typical of anorexics. She puts a cup of broccoli on a plate—the same plate every day—and places it on the couch under her arm, out of view. She slowly eats while watching *One Life to Live*, her favorite soap. She ponders yogurt and retrieves one from the freezer ("it's harder frozen, so you eat less"). By day's end she should have eaten 2,800 calories. But no one is watching over her, so she'll eat just 500.

The trailer is devoid of personal effects, save pictures of her family in heart-shaped frames. She points out a stuffed bunny left at her door by a college friend "who won't come in anymore because he can't stand to look at me." She notes that Prozac has helped her divorce herself from some elements of her past—for example, an obsessive neatness that kept her from allowing people to sit on her couch because "the cushions got squashed." But she still talks to her mother, an administrator at the university, four times a day.

Jayme says she used to go drinking every night with boyfriends until late in 1996, "when I lost the last forty pounds and scared them all away." Doesn't she want to date? "One of my main goals is to get married and have babies," she says brightly. But she hasn't had her period in 11 months, which causes her mother to say angrily, "I've come to accept the fact that I may never have grandchildren." Jayme has starved herself back into childhood—her skin is covered with lanugo, the hair infants are born with—and forward into old age. Her hair is thinning, her teeth are rotting, and the longer she goes without menstruating the more she risks bone decay. She is trapped between her future and her past.

Sisters with a Drive to Succeed

Jayme and her 23-year-old sister, Julie, grew up in Agra, an Oklahoma town that once had high hopes. Agra expected to become the site of a large freight center, and in the 1920s, a town of banks, saloons, cotton gins and 1,000 residents sprouted in the middle of nowhere. But the freight center was located elsewhere, and by the 1970s, when Julie and Jayme were born into what had become the typical Agra home—a trailer—all that was left was a blind man's concession stand, three churches, a school with 10 children per grade, and a population of 336. The only nightlife could be found in tin-shack bars. It was the smallest of small towns, the last place some might expect to find eating disorders, which have been tagged "rich kids' diseases."

But studies indicate that bulimia is most common among the lower classes and that anorexia occurs all over the U.S. The drive to succeed can play a more crucial role in the disorders than class or location, doctors think. Certainly, the Porters had drive. The girls' father, Galen Porter, a construction supervisor who raised livestock and prided himself on "always having fun," even during his tour in Vietnam, served on the local and state school boards. When Agra made national news after a parent demanded that the novel *The Color Purple* be taken off school shelves, Galen voted against censorship. He and his wife, Kay, sheltered their children from the more prohibitive local customs—which included a town church's demands that women stay at home, marry young and never cut their hair—and encouraged them to succeed.

Succeed Julie and Jayme did. Agra's school had no arts and few sports programs, but it did have 4-H, Future Farmers of America and Future Homemakers of America. Julie traveled the state with these organizations, winning speech contests while Jayme won sheep-showing contests. Both their bedrooms became shrines to achievement, their shelves stacked with trophies as tall as the pipes of a church organ. Both became one of only two in their grades to go to college.

Trouble hit when they were juniors in college. Their parents believe that for Julie, the discovery she wasn't going to be sorority president was the trigger: She lost 40 pounds in two months and landed in a hospital weighing 87 pounds. For Jayme, three years younger, her parents think it may have been the realization she hadn't excelled at anything since 4-H days. Both girls describe that period simply: "I had to be thinnest." As the last of their high school friends married, it was clear the sisters' ambition had spun out of control.

Treatment Takes Money

Julie was lucky. Although her mother's insurance policy picked up only $10,500 of the $73,000 bill for her nine-month stay at nearby Laureate Hospital, she was able to continue treatment because a bureaucratic error led Laureate to believe that welfare had taken up the slack. Even after the error was realized, Laureate let her stay on, swallowing more than $20,000.

Jayme was not so lucky. When she hit 90 pounds in January 1997, Laureate refused to take her unless her parents paid the $35,000 balance on Julie's bill. Hearing of a program in Arizona called Remuda Ranch, Kay and Galen say they checked with a benefits coordinator who told them their insurance company, American Fidelity Assurance, would not provide more than $10,000. So they remortgaged their house to come up with an extra $23,000 to pay for 60 days. But Jayme would stay in Arizona only 35 days. Remuda told the Porters Jayme had to leave immediately because she was considered "noncompliant."

At home over the next few weeks, Jayme lost more weight. "There was no place else to go," says Kay. Then, suddenly, hope: Wichita's Dr. Pryor consented to treat Jayme first and fight the insurance company later. Pryor, who had been cured of anorexia at age 15, took one look at Jayme and checked her into the hospital's intensive care unit.

Jayme continued her downward spiral. Her weight dropped to 60 pounds, and she was in a state of hypothermia with a body temperature below 92°. Within days, Pryor, fearing Jayme would die, called the family to her bedside. "She couldn't lift the sheets over herself," Kay recalls. "If she sat up, her heart rate would go to 180, then would slow to thirty-two beats a minute, and when she tried to get out of bed, it went off the charts. The nurses said you could see the outlines of her organs through her skin. Galen or I would sleep with her every night. We were terrified that if we left her she would die." Julie says she couldn't look at her sister: "I thought I'd be sick. I've seen skinny, skinny girls but nothing like that. She said she wanted a Mr. Potato Head, so I brought her one, but she couldn't even stick the little pieces in him."

Jayme pulled through with feeding tubes and was admitted to the psychiatric ward. She began sessions with Pryor. But after three weeks hope fizzled again. "They couldn't afford us, and we couldn't afford them anymore," says Pryor. Having racked up a $50,000 bill in Wichita, none of which American Fidelity paid, Jayme was released on April 23, 1997, weighing 79 pounds.

A Bias Against Eating Disorders

Insurance company officials would not comment on the adequacy of their policy, but they did provide records showing that American Fidelity paid only $30,000 of the $180,000 in psychiatric bills hospitals charged them. Pryor, whose program has since closed, was upset she had to release Jayme. "We should be able to keep them in the hospital for weeks after they've achieved ideal body weight, so we can begin to control behavior," she says. "In 1994 the average inpatient stay of an anorexic here was twenty-one days—now it's two to four days. Patients are coming in so much sicker it's frightening. I've been notorious for forcing the hospital to swallow bills. That's no way to run a program. It's the craziest thing in the world."

In May 1997, a month after Jayme was released, the nation's top eating disorders specialists gathered at the annual convention of the American Psychiatric Association in San Diego. They had a new problem. The National Alliance for the Mentally Ill (NAMI) was lobbying for bills in 37 states that would require insurers to treat mental illnesses as seriously as physical illnesses. But NAMI hadn't recommended including eating disorders in any of the parity bills. So the doctors planned to take on both the insurance industry and their own profession. They would try to persuade NAMI to include eating disorders in its legislation.

"There's such bias," explained Illinois eating disorders expert Dr. Pat Santucci. "A congressman asked me, 'How am I supposed to convince a small-business man he has to pay for this girlie disease?'" NAMI postponed the meeting. About the bills, NAMI later explained, it can't risk combating the prejudices until the biology of these illnesses is better understood. Anorexia doctors can't afford many of their own patients, let alone their own lobbyists. They had to wait and watch as bills excluding eating disorders were passed in several states.

A Family Divided: A Health Care Victim

It's summer, and Jayme sits in her trailer, eyeing the clock like an alcoholic before cocktail hour. When it's time for her workout, she says, "Yes!" and leaps out of her slouch with arms and legs akimbo, like a puppet jerked to life.

No matter how anorexia begins, many doctors believe that starvation and compulsive exercising become addictive, and this is clearly true for Jayme. At the OSU gym, she sits in a machine that's twice as big as she is, working out with weights as heavy as she is, for nearly two hours. "I'm so strong," she says proudly.

Sixty miles away, in her Tulsa home, Julie flops into a chair, looking as puppetlike as her sister. But resemblances to Jayme end there. Julie received six months of intensive treatment—group therapy, psychotherapy, nutrition and body image class, Alcoholics Anonymous

(AA), career counseling, 24-hour monitoring—and it changed her life. She lost her rituals, lost her need to please the world. Her house is as cheerfully unkempt as Jayme's is spartan. She graduated from college in June 1997 and has developed a love she picked up at the hospital—art therapy. Now she's considering getting a master's.

Kay and Galen, $145,000 in debt, have seen strange times. They have lost faith in doctors, who keep telling them their daughters' health is a commodity they must purchase. "I'm scared stiff for any of us to get sick now," Kay says. Both shift from affection to disbelief when they speak of their girls, trying to recall which qualities which daughter has lost to her disease. The sisters say their parents can pretend their problems don't exist. And the family's dynamics have changed dramatically. Just when Julie and her parents should have been mending fences after her illness, Jayme began going through the same thing, distracting Kay and Galen's attention. Hurt, Julie rarely comes home. The lack of outside resources has made Jayme more dependent on her parents than ever, reflected in the sardonic tone she adopts when speaking to them. ("I'm just a manipulative little girl, aren't I, Mommy?" she says at one point, wrapping her arms around Kay's neck.) The girls, who have had to compete for attention and money, almost never speak to each other.

The Porters were once a family of go-getters who worked and played hard together. Now Kay and Galen sometimes act like kids wondering where the fun has gone. The sisters often act like parents exasperated with the children; the parents, who lie in bed every night wondering what they did wrong, have been rendered as emotionally and financially helpless as their girls. The Porters are as trapped in their love for one another as they are trapped in the clutches of a disease—and a flawed health care system—they don't understand.

Julie will likely survive, which becomes evident when she talks about her weight. "Ninety-eight pounds," she says, though she doesn't like to admit it "because it's still too thin." Jayme, too, is afraid to reveal her weight, 81 pounds, but for a different reason: "It's not thin enough."

Fighting Back

Sarah Love finally got a break. After eight years of being released from hospitals prematurely because her insurance wouldn't cover long-term stays, the 22-year-old Tennessean was admitted to New York City's Columbia Presbyterian Medical Center in 1997 weighing 60 pounds. The catch: The free, months-long research program, funded largely by the New York State Psychiatric Institute, admits only 30 patients a year. Though Love gained 48 pounds, reaching and maintaining her top weight since she was 14, this is not an option for thousands of others suffering from anorexia and bulimia, unable to pay for their care.

Two recent New York cases, in which judges ordered Travelers and

Blue Cross to pay for the extended hospitalizations of anorexics, offer hope. Arguing that anorexia is a mental illness, the insurers had covered only 30 days of inpatient psychiatric care. But the judges said the eating disorder is a physical as well as mental condition and must be covered by medical benefits until a healthy weight is reached. The suits, though not legally binding, are promising, say doctors, who advise anorexics to use medical benefits for their treatment. The National Association of Anorexia Nervosa and Associated Disorders in Highland Park, Ill., which offers free advice on appealing insurers' rulings both in court and to state insurance commissioners, is looking for patients willing to join a possible class-action case. (Suits by individuals are rare—in part because the federal Employee Retirement Income Security Act of 1974 (ERISA) statute bars more than half the nation's employees from suing insurers for punitive damages or large malpractice sums; in part because eating disorders bankrupt people, fast.)

The Academy, an association of eating disorders experts, urges people to support bills that would change ERISA and include anorexia and bulimia in mental health parity laws. "Think of drive-through deliveries," says the Academy's Dr. Arnold Andersen. "Public outrage ignited bonfires."

CHAPTER 4

LIVING WITH AN EATING DISORDER: PERSONAL NARRATIVES

Contemporary Issues
Companion

HOOKED ON FOOD: A BULIMIC'S STORY

Kelly, as told to Sandy Fertman

In the following selection, a young woman using the pseudonym "Kelly" recounts her struggle with bulimia. She tells how she learned the purging that over time became a secret habit she could not control. Her "problem," Kelly explains, began to take total control of her life, causing her to tell one lie after another to protect her secret. She admits that even a heart attack was not enough to make her fight her bulimia. Finally, Kelly relates, intervention by her friends and a third heart attack made her realize that she had to stop bingeing and purging for good. Kelly's story is chronicled by writer Sandy Fertman.

I guess I'd say I had a pretty normal childhood.

I grew up in a house in California with my older brother, Jackson, and my identical twin sister, Carey. My sister and I have always been really close, but it's hard not to be when you're identical twins. My father is a psychologist and my mom owns a travel agency, but they were separated when I was about five. Carey, Jackson and I lived with our mom. Still, my dad has always been very much a part of my life.

My mom has always been overweight. I think her fears of us getting fat were instilled in us, even though she never voiced them. I first became aware of my own weight when I was around 15. One day, I looked in the mirror and noticed my face was changing. It looked kind of heavy and I thought, "Oh, my God! I have to lose weight!" It just hit me like a punch in the stomach.

From age seven, I had been a gymnast. I wasn't thin, but I always had to be aware of my body. But by the time I was 15, I was also modeling and acting, so I really had to start watching my weight.

The Family Secret

I had this diet of eating only steamed vegetables. One night, I ate too many vegetables and felt really sick. My mom said, "Oh, Kelly, just throw up." I said, "No way! That's so disgusting!" Mom said calmly, "Just do it, Kelly. You'll feel better." She told me to just stick my finger

Reprinted from "Real-Life True Story: Bulimia Almost Killed Me," as told to Sandy Fertman, *Teen* magazine, January 1997, with permission.

down my throat. So I did and after that, it became a habit, a really long, bad habit.

I felt a sense of power after that first time I purged. I thought I felt great that first night.

Both my sister and I learned how to purge that way. Carey and I would even throw up at the same time! We didn't think there was anything wrong with it. My mom knew the first couple of times, but then we decided we'd keep it our secret.

That secret lasted five years. I thought I'd kept it a secret from my friends, but later I found out they all knew. Your friends always know. They see how much you eat and you think you're being sneaky, saying you exercise a lot or that you have a fast metabolism. But after you come out of the bathroom and your face is all puffy, your eyes watery and your nose runny, they know what's going on. They just didn't have a clue what to do about it.

Living a Lie

My sister and I didn't really talk about our purging, but we both understood that if we ate a lot at any meal, we'd both have to sneak out and 'get rid of it.' After dinner at home, I'd usually run a bath to disguise the noise of vomiting. If I couldn't find a bathroom, I'd drive somewhere and get rid of it—in a bathroom, the bushes, wherever. At parties, I'd just 'get sick' in the bathroom after eating a lot of snacks. I usually could do it faster than someone could go to the bathroom! I'd eat until I was uncomfortable and then just go get rid of it.

My problem began to take total control of my life, because all I did all the time was try to figure out ways to eat a lot and how I was going to get rid of it. That's what your entire life is about. You make sure you won't even get into a situation where you can't throw up. So you end up planning your life around your eating and vomiting and it ends up controlling you. I avoided all camping trips, boat trips, excursions, even sleeping over at friends' houses just so I could eat and purge. It's a nightmare. You constantly have to sneak around, change your plans, lie. I'd plan ahead all of my excuses to allow me to stay in the bathroom when I went out to dinner with friends, making up things like, "There was a long line" or quickly slapping on some lipstick and saying, "Oh, I just had to retouch my makeup." You're always lying. It's sick.

I hardly ever ate fatty foods, because I was still watching my weight, but a few times a week I'd say, "Well, I can eat anything I want!" so I'd eat a donut or two and then purge. I got a lot of attention from being thin and at the time, that made it all worth it to me. In fact, most bulimic girls are never obese; they're usually average in weight, but want to have that 'edge' over other girls. I felt inferior to everyone else, so I'd think, 'If I can only have control over this one thing, I'll be able to make up for all my deficiencies.'

Obviously, I didn't have much of a sense of self-worth and truly didn't like myself a lot, never thinking I was smart enough, pretty enough or funny enough. You feel like you're not worthy of being loved or even liked. So you get into this self-destructive behavior, thinking that if you're thin, it will compensate for all your inadequacies. But even though you think you've got it under control, you're way out of control!

The worst feeling was that I felt like a fraud all the time, always keeping this secret, hiding this habit. I was so ashamed. It's such a secret that your whole life becomes centered around keeping it. I chose friends that could never get close to me, because if they did, they'd figure out my little secret. In my case, though, I was lucky to still have my childhood friends, but the people I really began to hang out with were very emotionally detached and distant people. That's what I wanted.

During the whole time I was eating and purging, I never had a boyfriend. I didn't feel lovable; I figured no one would want me. I dated a lot, but even to this day, I haven't gotten serious with anyone. I was very social, but it was always very superficial, like going to dances and hanging out with large groups of friends, nothing intimate. It was really easy to hide my problem from the guys I dated, because no one assumes you're going to the bathroom to vomit. . . .

I was always faking it, always full of lies and excuses to enable me to keep my secret. I'd say to my friends, "Oh, I've gotta get going" or "I've gotta run some errands," nonspecific excuses so I could go munch out and throw up. Your life revolves around eating. It got to a point where I didn't need to use my finger or anything. My muscles just did it.

Lying all the time made me feel terrible about myself. I knew I had a serious problem if I had to deceive people all the time to keep it up. You realize you're trapped, but it's literally the most important thing in your life. My best friend knew about it; in fact, all my closest friends did and they'd talk to me about it, but they couldn't change me. Sometimes they'd just walk away, but since they're friends for life, they eventually came back. In that way, I was incredibly fortunate.

Eating Me Up Inside

I was always an A student, but during my senior year, I got kicked out of high school. I simply lost interest in school and everything about it. I was just so bored and I had started hanging out with this group of friends outside of school who I called 'the low-lifes.' I just didn't care about anything anymore, except my habit, of course.

Things went from bad to worse that year. By then, I was throwing up six times a day, every day. One afternoon, I was sitting in traffic school and I suddenly got this tingling feeling in my hands and then my muscles started contracting and curling up and contorting. My whole body just froze! I excused myself and went to the pay phone to get help and when I started walking back, I screamed, "Oh, my God!!" and I collapsed on the floor by the classroom—my legs were paralyzed. I couldn't move any of my muscles, even my tongue! My mom came to get me and said we'd wait until the morning to see how I felt. I said, "Mom, I may not be alive in the morning!" so she drove straight to the emergency room.

The doctor examining me told us I had had a minor heart attack. He explained that I had hardly any electrolytes left in my body from throwing up so much. Those minerals maintain your heart and muscle activity, basically everything. My mom, of course, had known I was bulimic, but now she, too, had to face up to it. The nurses immediately injected my vein with a needle and hooked me up to this potassium drip. It was the worst pain I have ever felt in my life, like razor blades going through every vein in my body! You can feel it going into your arms, your shoulders, your heart, your stomach, your thighs, your legs and your feet. It's like someone is taking razor blades soaked in salt and alcohol and dragging them slowly through your body. I was crying through the whole procedure, "Please stop it! Please, please!" But it was either that or I'd die. . . .

I stayed overnight in the hospital and you'd think I would have learned my lesson, but I didn't. I started throwing up right afterward. I felt like the alternative to purging was getting fat and I really believed that was worse than having a heart attack!

Everyone told me I had to see a therapist, so I went to a counseling group at the local university medical center for a short time.

Friends to the Rescue

My true friends decided it was time to take action, so they did an 'intervention.' That's when your friends and family get together and confront you all at once with your problem. My sister and four friends showed up at my house and all day long they kept saying, "Kelly, you're so smart and so beautiful; you don't need to do this!" They said they just didn't understand how I could do this to myself, basically letting me know how much it was hurting them. I felt like I was really disappointing them, like something was really abnormal about me. That's what really made me feel like I had to do something about my bulimia; I felt so incredibly ashamed.

The intervention was actually wonderful because my secret was finally lifted off of my shoulders. As painful as it was to be told I was, in a way, a failure, it was good for me. I realized I needed help.

At that time, I looked so strange because of my problem. My face became a 'moon face'—kind of puffy and round—which is pretty common with bulimics, my teeth had decayed from the acids of regurgitating, my eyes were kind of filmy and my hair had started falling out. Starting to eat normally again was incredibly hard. It was hard to start digesting again. You almost have to eat all liquids at first. I started swelling so badly for about 24 hours after eating that the doctors put me on a diuretic [that's a medication to get rid of the excess water] and other medications for digestion.

After that intervention, I stopped purging. By that time, Carey was already going to group and individual counseling and was taking medication to treat her bulimia. I never did any of that. But only a year later, I started throwing up again. I hadn't broken the habit. I ended up having another minor heart attack while I was driving home from the gym one day. Even at the hospital while I was getting that horrible potassium drip, I was wondering, "How can I keep eating and getting rid of it without dying?" I can't believe that I was that out of control!

Just one week later, I was back in the hospital with another heart attack and that's when I thought, "Oh, my God! I can't control this!" That's when I decided to stop it for good.

Filling Myself Up

It's been three years now and I feel great. Although I've never gone to therapy, I do talk to another recovering bulimic about it. I knew I didn't want to die and I started realizing who I was and that I really did like myself.

I took the proficiency test to graduate from high school and then went on to graduate from the local university magna cum laude. Now I have my own television production company and I'm producing an outdoor-related TV series. I really love my work. Actually, most bulimics are very ambitious people. They're into that 'control thing' so they know what they want and are inspired to go to extremes to get it—not that that's always good.

My whole life has changed without the pressure of hiding a secret and supporting a habit. All of a sudden, you have an empty part of your life you have to fill. It's like when you end a relationship with a boyfriend: You've been seeing him and then all of a sudden he's not there anymore. That's what I'm doing now. Battling bulimia was the bravest thing I've ever done. Now I have to face those fears of 'getting big' and having no one like me. Today, I'm 15 pounds heavier than I was when I was bulimic, but I think I'm in good shape. And most importantly, I'm really happy.

Food for Thought

If you're starting to binge and purge, you aren't in control just because you're controlling your weight. Actually, you're way out of control. Once you start purging, it's like cigarettes. It's a hard habit to break. It's with you for years, maybe even a lifetime. You think you can stop any time, but your fear of getting fat is so overwhelming that you're driven to this extreme behavior. And even if you think it's your little secret, it's not! You're not fooling anyone! People close to you know.

Definitely talk to someone about your feelings. Confide in your good friends. If you're close to your parents and you have an open relationship with them, talk to them. You can also go to a 12-step program, such as Overeaters Anonymous. Or you can go to an eating disorder clinic or see a therapist or a counselor. But make sure you talk to someone before it's too late. Bulimia can kill you. I know. It almost killed me.

MY DAUGHTER, MY MOTHER: OUR STRUGGLE WITH EATING DISORDERS

Rebecca Cohen and Tobin Levy

Rebecca Cohen is a writer and contributing editor to *House and Garden* magazine. In the following selection, she and her daughter, Tobin Levy, express their feelings about their struggle with Levy's anorexia and bulimia—and with each other. According to Cohen, Levy's eating disorders nearly destroyed their relationship and put Levy in mortal danger. According to Levy, her mother did not always give her the support or affection she needed. What scared her most, Levy admits, was the realization that recovery was all up to her. Cohen acknowledges that she is optimistic about the future but still questions whether Levy, or anyone else, ever recovers fully from an eating disorder.

Rebecca Cohen: My 22-year-old daughter Tobin frowned when I suggested we collaborate on an article about her eating disorder. She looked at me as if to say "What do you know about it?" What I know is that the disease nearly destroyed our relationship, and that Tobin could have died from any number of complications brought about by 10 years of anorexia and bulimia, including malnutrition, kidney failure, gastrointestinal problems or even a heart attack. What I wanted to understand was the part I played in her illness and recovery.

Tobin used to be pudgy. She said the girls in her fifth grade class made fun of her and paired her with the chubby boys in their boyfriend-girlfriend games. At nearly 5½ feet tall by the end of the sixth grade, Tobin stood apart from her mostly small classmates. I blamed teachers and classmates for her unhappiness. She blamed her weight and began eating ever decreasing portions of food.

Her strategy worked. By the time she was 12, Tobin sported a newly lean frame. She had prominent cheekbones and a hollow, unhappy look. My friends noticed before I did that she was too thin. I naively explained that my daughter was just trying to feel better about herself by becoming fashionably slender.

Tobin Levy: The summer after sixth grade I went on my first diet. I was excited that I could get down to 101 pounds. All my friends' bod-

Reprinted from Rebecca Cohen and Tobin Levy, "Overcoming an Eating Disorder," *American Health for Women*, October 1997, by permission of Reader's Digest Publications.

ies were changing that year. Some girls had breasts and curvy hips. Some were still tiny, while others grew tall. All I wanted was to be thin. Thin, so I would be pretty. Pretty, so my friends would like me and my family would be proud. Everyone told me how great I looked except my mother. Maybe she was jealous.

"Eat something—anything," she would say as she handed me a banana and some buttered toast.

"No!" I'd scream. I'd take the food and trash it the minute she looked away. When Mom caught on to that trick, she'd make me take bites of things before she'd let me leave for school. I'd chew, then spit the food out as soon as she was out of sight. She just didn't understand what it was like to be fat.

During seventh grade I learned about bulimia from watching my friends' big sisters experiment with diets. They told me how they binged and purged in order to lose weight. It seemed pretty simple. I would do it only for a little while, I thought. But over a year later, I was throwing up 20 or 30 times a day. It had become effortless, like breathing or blinking. Quitting wasn't going to be as easy as I thought.

When I read an article about how bulimia can destroy the esophagus and weaken the heart, I got scared. Instead of offering help, my mother tried to bully me into eating better. She frequently screamed at me about how she was tired of finding the toilet splattered with vomit. During this time she also made frequent trips to the grocery store for chips, ice cream, milk, cereal and other food on which I would binge. My twin sister and older sister didn't know how to deal with my behavior. It scared and angered them. My father, often preoccupied with work, wasn't aware of what was going on. At least he didn't ask. And I continued to throw up, only now I did it as a way of getting back at all of them. It became a game to see how often I could throw up in the sink when my mother turned her back.

Getting Help

Rebecca: I missed the sweet-smelling little girl who had cuddled with me in the morning before she was old enough to go to school. Instead I got arguments over hairstyles and whether she should wear shorts or a dress to elementary school. These disputes had been manageable, but when she was a teenager, the arguments got even more frustrating, as Tobin continually agonized over her appearance and weight.

"Do I look fat?" was her first question each morning. There was no right answer. If I teased her and said, "Yes," there would be tears and hysteria. If I told her she didn't look fat, she would accuse me of lying to her. If I refused to answer, she would respond, "You don't care."

Both of her sisters told me I should make her stop throwing up. They insisted I had the power to do this, although neither of them ever listened to me. Instead I found her a new psychiatrist. We all had already seen a long list of therapists. One child was acting up, another acting out; I was depressed, and my husband and I—small wonder—weren't getting along. But despite therapy, Tobin's obsession with her weight continued, and by the time she was 16 her physical health was in jeopardy. She had tooth decay, pale skin, thinning hair, and—although I didn't know it then—occasional heart palpitations brought on by bulimia.

Tobin: At 16, after nearly five years of individual therapy, bingeing, purging and occasional bouts of anorexia, I decided to enter the inpatient eating disorder program at a local hospital. I was nervous and scared. "Maybe you should wait so you don't have to miss any of your junior year," my mother said. "Let's find an outpatient program that will take up less of your time."

Wait? I had already waited about five years. All I needed was for her to support my decision. I had taken the initiative, and now it seemed she didn't want me to get better. We fought all the way to the hospital.

An Inpatient Program

Rebecca: Taking Tobin to the inpatient program felt like publicly confessing my personal failure as a mother. If she'd been hit by a truck, I would have run with her in my arms to the nearest hospital. So why hold back now? Perhaps I blamed myself and didn't want to face my own culpability. Maybe her illness was caused by my not being supportive enough, as she claimed; by my always being at odds with her father; by my always working instead of being available to listen. Of course, it didn't really matter by then. She had asked for help, and her father and I should have supported her. Instead we kept putting off her best hope for recovery. We argued about the embarrassment of people finding out and against disrupting the school year.

Tobin: The hospital had white walls and green towels, and it smelled of antiseptic. I couldn't believe I was there. I didn't look sick and I hadn't experienced any of the sexual or physical trauma that I knew were common among people with eating disorders. But my uncertainty lasted only a day. The women in the program welcomed me as if I were an old friend. We shared our most painful experiences, cried and comforted each other with hugs. This place that had initially felt like a prison became a safe haven I was afraid to leave.

My day began at 7:30 a.m. when the nurse woke me, weighed me and checked my stats. I was busy all day with group therapy, family therapy, spirituality sessions, and nutrition and body image classes. The hardest parts of the day were mealtimes. I could read the struggle in everyone's face, feel it in my own stomach. They gave me a meal plan made up of normal food in bigger portions than I had been eating, and I had to finish at least 90% of what was on my plate at every meal. After meals I wanted more than anything to rid myself of what I'd eaten, but the program was structured so that someone was with me at all times, so I couldn't throw up my food.

The meal plan allowed me to stay healthy and maintain a weight that was acceptable to me and my doctors. If I followed the plan, I knew that I wouldn't be undereating or overeating and that I didn't have to feel guilty. I thought that as long as I held on to the plan I would never be sick again.

Rebecca: After two weeks, Tobin left the hospital. But at home she was afraid to let go of the strict diet that the hospital's nutritionist prescribed for her. Her rigidity made me nervous—she was still obsessed with controlling her food intake and weight. But in spite of this continued obsession with food, her attitude improved significantly. As her sense of humor and sharp intellect awakened, I realized the enormous toll the disease had taken on her during the preceding years. Unfortunately, what I thought to be a cure was merely a cease-fire in the hostilities between Tobin and her own body, and between my daughter and me.

A Brief Cease-Fire

Tobin: Although there were still days when I struggled, by my senior year of high school I had survived almost a year of abstinence from throwing up. My mother acknowledged the value of the hospital program and apologized for not being initially supportive. We could talk without animosity about normal things: boys, school and my plans for college. It was wonderful. At the same time, I was working with other kids in my school who struggled with eating disorders, and I even gave a speech on the subject to the whole student body.

But toward the end of senior year, the cycle began again, and this time my relationship with my mother became even more strained. After nearly 25 years of marriage, my parents announced they were getting a divorce. Was it my fault? My stay in the hospital had certainly led to an increase in therapy sessions for various members of the family. Maybe if I hadn't caused so many problems, they would have stayed together. I felt sad and guilty, as if my whole family should blame me for what was happening. The result? I started losing weight again.

Rebecca: Tobin was accepted to Barnard College in New York City. Her application was full of references to strong young women and feminist ideals. But life at home was not so good. Although Tobin mouthed acceptance of the divorce, her body let her father and me know how unhappy she was. She was getting thinner and had to visit her internist throughout the summer because of gastrointestinal aches and pains, a result of the recurring bulimia.

Helping her pack for college was agonizing. That June I had moved out of our family home and into a small house of my own, but at my daughter's request I returned day after day to help box her things. She was hostile. I was hostile. Teary-eyed, I said good-bye, but I guiltily welcomed the separation. I needed to take care of myself for awhile.

Tobin called often from college and wrote that her grades were good, but that she wasn't making friends easily, nor was she dating. I blamed the city, the school and insensitive classmates for Tobin's unhappiness before finally admitting that the eating disorder had returned.

Challenges at College

Tobin: My first year at college didn't go as planned. I had no boyfriend and few girlfriends—no way to relax. My mother would write or call me almost every day, giving advice on how to make college better. It seemed clear that she wanted to feel needed after the divorce. I felt like she was grabbing on to me, her baby. Finally, pressure from school and home took their toll. I focused once again on the thing I was good at controlling: my weight. By the end of freshman year, I was 5' 9" and weighed 118 pounds. While studying in Spain the next summer, I lost another 10 pounds. I came home tan and happy, thinking I looked great. My friends thought differently; they stopped talking to me, thinking it would force me to confront my illness.

Rebecca: Tobin was devastated when her friends stopped speaking to her. I tried to console her, saying the self-confidence she'd experienced in Europe was more important than the weight loss. I was in denial again. Her internist warned that she would need medical care. He was right. She went back to school with medicine to ease what we all assumed was an ulcer.

Tobin: I returned to school sophomore year knowing it was the one place where I could be as thin as I wanted. I ate even less and exercised more. Nobody even noticed. The letters and phone calls from my mother slowed to a trickle. She had started dating her current husband and had developed her own life. I thought she didn't need me anymore. My weight dropped to 101 pounds, and studying became increasingly difficult as my depression worsened.

Rebecca: How could my daughter think I didn't care? Whenever we were on the phone, I would listen to her describe one traumatic event after another. She would hang up relieved, while I carried the weight of her depression around for the rest of the day. One night while she was visiting her older sister in Philadelphia, she went to the emergency room because of intense stomach pains. She and her sister called me long distance every hour for advice. Tobin was scared, but she insisted on returning to school. I immediately made arrangements to join her in New York. We visited the student health center together to check out the eating disorder resources there. I found her a nutritionist and a psychotherapist who specialized in eating disorders. But I had to return to my own life, leaving Tobin to struggle through the fall semester.

Tobin: Second semester sophomore year, I couldn't study anymore. I was sick of not eating, sick of measuring out my food, sick of being unhappy and crying all the time. I was so sick of everything that the only thing left was to be physically sick again. And I was.

Rebecca: By February Tobin was calling every night and sobbing on the phone, depressed and unable to function. I finally intervened and ordered her to leave school during the middle of spring semester. Then I went to New York to pack up her dorm room and ship her belongings home. I was scared. I was being given one last chance to save my daughter, and I didn't have any idea how to proceed.

Facing Facts

Tobin: I moved in with my mother and her future husband. At first I was so embarrassed, I refused to leave the house. I had let everyone down. I spent my time bingeing on whatever was in the pantry and throwing up in the kitchen sink while my mother worked in the next room.

I tried the hospital eating disorder program again, this time as an outpatient, looking as always for something or someone else to fix me. But I had already learned everything they could teach about nutrition, family dynamics and body image. So I stopped going after three weeks. It was all up to me now, and that scared me the most. But it was a turning point.

Rebecca: When Tobin came home, we began to talk frankly about her disease. At first she was angry, accusatory and said I didn't understand. I didn't. Despite countless hours of therapy—in large groups while she was hospitalized, family counseling and sessions with my own therapist—I still can't comprehend how a bright and beautiful young woman can be so self-destructive and insecure. Like any mother who helplessly watches her child struggle, I wonder why my daughter has to suffer.

Tobin: After about three months, I moved out of my mother's house into an apartment by myself and began working full-time at a clothing store, going out for coffee with friends and going dancing. I started doing special things for myself like buying candles, taking bubble baths and listening to my favorite music. Slowly but surely, I replaced the time I'd spent hurting myself by being nice to myself. This helped get the bulimia under control.

Thinking about my relationship with my twin sister on my own and through therapy has also helped. Growing up, I was always thinner than she was, and it was clear to me that people differentiated us only by our weight. The message we continually received was that the thinner you were, the more beautiful you were. She hurt, and I wanted to hurt myself. I wanted to throw up her pain, their comments and my anger and guilt for being the thin one.

Hope and Change

Rebecca: My twin daughters can't seem to help looking to each other for cues on how to behave. When one is heavy, the other responds by losing weight. When one has split ends, the other gets her hair neatly trimmed. The line that separates these two distinct human beings often seems blurred.

Tobin credits a whole series of events—her insight on her relationship with her twin sister, moving to her own apartment, leaving school temporarily, making new friendships and repairing old ones—with helping her become more comfortable with her body. Writing about these last 11 years has shaken up our relationship a bit, triggered more tears, but it has also helped smooth a path toward a more peaceful future for both of us.

Tobin: Up until last year, I was a completely different person; I was fragile, afraid to make mistakes, unable to speak my mind. Now I've found my voice again. I'm attractive, outspoken and energetic. I can even take pride in my lack of perfection—exercising three days a week instead of seven, getting a B instead of an A and being a size 8 instead of a size 4. I haven't stopped throwing up completely, but it doesn't control my life as it has in the past. But when I'm alone, especially at night, I still have a hard time. I've been struggling with this eating disorder for half my life, and I'm scared to death of the behavior recurring.

Rebecca: Does anybody fully recover from an eating disorder? I don't know. My daughter takes pride in her accomplishments now, but somehow it's not enough for her. Tobin craves external validation that she's attractive, and to her that means being thin. After all these years, she still asks The Question every time I see her: "Do I look fat?" In fact, she asked me that just the other day.

"No," I answered honestly.

"Are you sure?"

"You look terrific, and don't ask again!" (Will she ever move beyond this obsession with body weight?)

My daughter held her head high, struck a pose and said, "I do look pretty good today, don't I?"

It's taken her 22 years to learn to say those words. I'm optimistic.

FROM EXCESS BAGGAGE TO SELF-LOVE AND PEACE

Crystal J. Phillips, with Deborah Gregory

In the following selection, pharmaceutical sales representative Crystal J. Phillips relates how she stopped using food for comfort and achieved a major weight loss and a new outlook on life. Phillips describes the negative forces in her life—from the slow death of a brother from AIDS to the destruction of her parents' home by a hurricane to her own illness and failed marriage—and explains how they overwhelmed her to the point that she lost control of her eating. Not until she reached "an emotional, physical and spiritual rock bottom," Phillips confesses, did she start to turn around her life. Deborah Gregory is a contributing writer for *Essence*, a lifestyle magazine for African-American women.

January 1, 1995. Here I am at 245 pounds trying to get down to 133. Am I fooling myself or what? I feel huge! I went to church and asked God to help me get down to the fabulous weight I know I can achieve.

I wrote those words two and a half years ago when I woke up to the harsh reality that I was carrying 245 pounds on my five-foot four-inch frame. I weigh more than Mike Tyson, but I was no heavyweight boxing champion. Like most things in life, the extra pounds didn't appear overnight. My out-of-control bingeing and weight problem were the culmination of personal crises and a lifelong struggle with low self-esteem.

The trying times took a turn for the worse seven years ago, when I got married. Deep inside I knew the union wasn't right, but I thought no one else would want me because I was heavy. Around the same period, my younger brother revealed that he was HIV-positive. While he was getting progressively sicker, my marriage began to fall apart. To cope, I developed a destructive routine: Every evening, after stopping by my brother's house to take care of him, I went to the grocery store to buy binge foods. My favorite feast consisted of a porterhouse steak with french fries, peach cobbler, potato chips and four pints of Haagen Dazs ice cream. Afterward, I would take Alka-Seltzer to soothe

Reprinted from Crystal J. Phillips and Deborah Gregory, "Weighting to Exhale," *Essence*, June 1997, by permission.

my stomach and gather all my binge-food evidence to put in a separate trash bag on the sidewalk.

When my husband began complaining about my weight, I joined a liquid-diet program and lost 43 pounds in three months. But once the fasting portion of the program was over, and my brother's health began deteriorating rapidly, I started overeating again.

Then in 1992 and 1993 a series of events sent my life into a tailspin. My cherished brother died at the age of 33. Two months later, Hurricane Andrew destroyed my parents' home in Miami. Just a few months after that, I found out I had fibroid tumors so large that the doctor had to perform a partial hysterectomy to remove them. I was left infertile, and my husband's attitude was, "What good are you to me now if you can't give me babies?" During that time, my bingeing was going full force, and I regained all the weight I had lost, plus more. In the spring of 1993, my favorite aunt died of an asthma attack, and I was beside myself with grief.

When I could no longer tolerate the pain of my marriage, I left my husband the following September, taking only my belongings, my brother's dog and the car. I moved into an apartment by myself in Towson, a suburb outside Baltimore, and continued to use food to push down deep feelings of loneliness and failure. It wasn't until 1995 that I finally hit an emotional, physical and spiritual rock bottom. I'd had enough. It was time to rejuvenate.

Healing the Pain Within

July 12, 1995. My eating is out of control. I only had two bananas to eat all day because I'm scared to eat. I worked from 8 in the morning to 8 at night. I'm stressed out about my job and about my weight.

The first step to my recovery was to go for a complete medical checkup. My physician, Dr. Dana Simpler, told me I had borderline high blood pressure. That diagnosis got my attention, and because both diabetes and breast cancer run in my family, I had other causes for concern.

To begin healing, I started praying, lighting candles and meditating every day. I also bought books on food addiction, nutrition and spiritual self-help, including Iyanla Vanzant's *Acts of Faith: Daily Meditations for People of Color*. Because I'm convinced that overeating is an addiction like alcohol, I read *Little Big Book*, which explains the 12-step recovery process. I could not have gained control of my food addiction had I not first surrendered my will to a higher power. It was through this act that I found some release from the desire to binge.

Another way I coped was by following a suggestion Oprah Winfrey made: I started writing down my thoughts and feelings in a journal. Looking back over my life, I noticed a pattern: Whenever the going got tough, I turned to food. I remembered back when I was the tallest and the biggest kid in my seventh-grade class, and because of my size

I was excluded from slumber parties and sexually harassed by boys. That was when I decided to become fat. Food became my shield of armor and source of consolation. It had been my comfort ever since.

During the first six months of journal writing, I let out all the pain and cried like a baby. I called my mother and shared with her, for the first time, all the secret resentments I had had as a child. I also started hugging myself that I loved me. This ritual felt strange at first, but the sentiment slowly started to sink in.

New Attitude, New Body

March 10, 1996. Today was a good-food day. For breakfast, I had a peach, two nonfat rolls and coffee. I don't really feel like exercising, but it's a nice spring day and my dog is used to going for his walk.

With the help of Dr. Simpler and an armful of nutrition books, I embarked on a new way of eating and exercising. I took out all the high-fat, high-sodium and high-sugar foods in my cupboards and gave them away. Because I had tried so many different weight-loss programs, I knew exactly what a basic healthy food plan should look like: three balanced, low-fat meals a day with snacks in between. I ate my last meal no later than 7:00 P.M., and I didn't bring any "trigger foods"—like fried chicken, ice cream, steak, potato chips—into the apartment. I ate in public where everyone could see me and only took small portions. I also dusted off my exercise equipment and started working out for an hour each day, combining 30 minutes of aerobics with 30 minutes of weight training.

Within a few months I had lost 32 pounds, and I was loving the process. For the first time in my life, I didn't concentrate on a goal weight or on what I would eat as soon as my diet was over. I was more concerned about changing my attitude toward food and exercise. Not only did I get a new attitude, but I also tried a new look, thanks to my sister, who supported me in my efforts to get healthy. She prodded me to get rid of the perm I'd been a slave to all my life and put my hair in braids. I was truly ready to embrace me.

When I got down to 187 pounds and the catcalls from anonymous men on the street corners began, I was frightened. It upset me, but instead of turning to food, I wrote about it in my journal.

In order to maintain recovery from a powerful addiction, it's also important to give something back. So for the past year, I've been running one-hour support-group meetings in my apartment every Saturday for women who want to reach a healthy weight and regain control of their lives. The groups are small—between ten and 15 women. The first thing I tell them is this is a place to be honest. I talk about my experience and offer motivation, then open the meeting for discussion. Each woman gets a chance to talk about her week and discuss what she ate. We then make a low-fat meal and eat it together. I later type up the recipe and hand it out the following week. Motivating other women motivates me, and the support we offer one another keeps us all on the healthy track.

As of today I've shed a total of 108 pounds. I have gone from a size 20 to a size 6 and lost one shoe size, three bra sizes, two ring sizes and one hat size! I now exercise six days a week and have completely removed beef, chicken and turkey from my diet. Because of my success, my mother has also gotten inspired and lost 40 pounds! Most important, I've lost all the negative baggage that once overwhelmed me—and in its place gained self-love and peace.

EXPERIENCES OF A MALE ANOREXIC

Michael Krasnow

Michael Krasnow began his ongoing struggle with anorexia in the mid-1980s. In the following selection from his book *My Life as a Male Anorexic*, Krasnow describes the onset of the disease that has affected his life for so many years. According to Krasnow, he had felt fat since he was eleven years old but did not become anorexic until he was a teenager. During his first year of high school, Krasnow relates, he became depressed and developed an obsession with studying. This obsession was replaced first with excessive toothbrushing and then with an obsession about his weight. The self-control he gained over his eating patterns and his intake made him feel special and all-powerful, Krasnow confides.

For some time now, my mother has been encouraging me to write a book about my screwed-up life and my experiences with anorexia nervosa and depression. I've never given this idea much consideration. Because of the depression, I just haven't had the motivation. However, now that I'm not working, I figure I may as well give it a shot. After all, it's been around two years since I stopped working; most of this time has been spent sitting in a chair in my apartment, staring at the wall. Talk about a waste. These past couple of years epitomize my life—a total waste.

First, the facts that make me an "official" anorexic. The so-called professionals, your $100-per-hour, know-it-all doctors, will list many symptoms and characteristics of anorexia. The bottom line is that I am 5'9" and feel fat, despite weighing only 75 pounds. Just for the record, I am white, American, Jewish, and twenty-five years old. I live in Hollywood, Florida, and . . . my name is Michael Krasnow. What sets me aside from most other anorexics is that I am male.

For years, anorexia existed, but very few people knew of it. Women who suffered from it did not realize that they were not alone. Eventually, as more became known and anorexia became more publicized, a greater number of women came forward to seek help, no longer feeling that they would be considered strange or outcasts from society.

Maybe with the publication of this book, more men with the problem will realize that they are not alone either, and that they do not suffer from a "woman's disease." They can come forward without worrying about embarrassment.

Who knows? Maybe as a result of this book, I'll end up on television. . . . The more publicity I can get, the better. Each book that is sold will make that many more people aware of the serious problem of male anorexia. And the more people that know, the more demand there will be to help those with this problem. . . .

So much for preliminaries. It is time to tell you about myself. . . .

Feelings of Being Fat

I suppose I had a typical childhood. Born in Rochester, New York, on April 27, 1969, I moved to Framingham, Massachusetts, when I was two months old and lived there for about twenty-two years. I enjoyed being with my friends and family, loved to read and play sports, had a hobby (comic books) and a newspaper route, watched TV, idolized Larry Bird and the Boston Celtics, and had no worries. I was an all-around average child. My one unusual characteristic was that I felt fat from as early as age eleven, when I was in the sixth grade. I occasionally mentioned this feeling to my parents and grandparents, but not with any seriousness. I used to joke with them that I was going to diet. Understandably, no one paid any attention. After all, I was of average weight. Actually, I was less than average, the type of child that others refer to as "so skinny."

When I speak of feeling fat, what I mean is that when I look down at my stomach, I see it as sticking out or being bloated. . . .

I started to wonder why I felt fat. I knew that statistically I wasn't fat, and everyone told me how skinny I was. I decided to try dieting, but never kept to it for more than a couple of days (I figured it was a lack of willpower). Because I never stuck to a diet, no one paid much attention.

At this time, my feelings of being fat began to affect my activities. Before, I had felt fat, but had not been influenced by these feelings. Now, I would not go to the beach because I did not want to take off my shirt. Without a shirt, I'd see my stomach and feel fat; I believed others who saw my stomach would also think I looked fat. When I could not make up an excuse for not going to the beach, I kept my shirt on, or if I had to take it off, I sucked in my gut and held it.

Sucking in my gut became a way of life. I played basketball in my temple's youth league. In practice, we scrimmaged as "shirts" and "skins." I hated being on the "skins" team. When I was, I was unable to focus on the game, being too preoccupied with thinking about sucking in my gut. . . .

My father was a member of a health club, Racquetball Five-O. . . . I went to this health club with my dad once or twice a week. When I was in the locker room, naked, I always sucked in my gut.

I am singling out these locker-room occasions because they lead to an interesting observation. Standing in that locker room, I saw the other men around me as being fat. In other words, I felt fat, but my disillusionment was not limited to myself. Most anorexics will see other people as being thin. I'm different; I also view other people as being fat, even if they aren't. If someone says that so-and-so is thin, I will frequently think otherwise. . . .

Depression and Obsessive Studying

It was at the start of my first year in high school, September 1983, that my "fat feelings" gained strength, and my troubles started. Oddly, it was strange behavior of a different sort that preceded the anorexia. As a freshman, I became obsessed with studying. . . .

On the very first day of school, I signed up to run on the cross-country track team. I was an okay runner. I improved a lot after that first day.

In the middle of October, my grandfather died after suffering from cancer for about two years. . . . It's true that his death coincided with the time that my depression and obsessive studying began, but as far as I'm concerned, it was just coincidence.

When the depression began, I quit the cross-country track team. I simply did not have the motivation. A month later, I tried out for and made the freshman basketball team. I sat on the bench 99 percent of the time and after about one month, my depression increased and the studying began to get out of hand. I quit basketball (I had already given up my newspaper route) and began to devote all my time to my school work.

I got home from school about 2:30 in the afternoon and studied until midnight. Soon, I was studying until 1:00 in the morning—then 2:00. Eventually, I started going to bed at 2:00 a.m. and setting my alarm for 4:00 a.m., so that I could study some more before school. I even studied on the fifteen-minute bus ride to school. . . .

The studying was probably part obsession, part perfection. Every piece of homework had to be immaculate. For instance, my math homework could not have one little erasure mark. This meant I might have to copy it over four, five, or six times. This perfection was very frustrating. To vent this frustration, I began banging my head against the wall. . . .

During these few months that my studying and depression worsened, I began to see a psychiatrist, Dr. C. . . .

Dr. C prescribed antidepressant medication. From 1984 until 1990, I was on and off different antidepressants (nortriptyline, imipramine, desipramine, amoxapine, amitriptyline, and Prozac). Since none of these ever helped or made any difference, there is no point in discussing each time I began a new one. . . .

My parents and Dr. C decided to withdraw me from school. They made the right decision. Deep down, I think wanted this to happen. By being out of school, I did not have the need to study. There was nothing I could do about it. Because had no control over the matter, I would not feel guilty for not studying. Once I was out of school, it was out of my hands. . . .

A New Obsession

When he took me out of school, Dr. C said that he had one main concern. He was worried that I would replace my obsession with studying with a new obsession. This possibility had never occurred to me until he mentioned it. Dr. C put the idea of a new obsession into my mind. As a result, when I left school, I found myself thinking, "Okay, Dr. C said I might end up with a new obsession; now, what can I do to replace the studying?" In other words, I made a conscious effort to find a new obsession. To this day, although I could be wrong, I truly believe that this would not have happened if Dr. C had not said anything.

What was this new obsession? It was toothbrushing. At first, I was brushing about two hours per day. Very soon, it was twelve hours per day. While either sitting in front of the television or walking around the house, I would brush, brush, brush. This lasted for only a couple of weeks (I went through a lot of toothpaste and a lot of toothbrushes), before I made the decision that would lead to the anorexia.

I really hated the toothbrushing. Who wouldn't? One day, I woke up and said to myself, "Oh, gee, I don't want to brush my teeth all day. Well, hey, don't have anything to eat, your mouth won't get dirty, and you won't have to brush." With this in mind, I didn't eat that day. I also did not eat (I did drink water) for the next three days.

Of course, Dr. C and my parents became extremely worried about my physical well-being. Finally, on June 16, 1984, I was admitted to Westwood Lodge, a psychiatric hospital in Westwood, Massachusetts. . . .

Upon being admitted, I was assigned to Dr. B. He was now the boss. I was through with Dr. C. I still refused to have anything but water. My vital signs became very bad. My blood pressure was so low that the nurse had trouble taking it. My temperature was below 96 degrees. . . .

My feelings about the hospital were similar to those I had when I was taken out of school. Deep down, I think that I wanted to be hospitalized. It was a relief. Again, it was a control issue. I had to eat—I thought I had no choice (in later years, I would realize that I had more control than I thought), but I couldn't brush my teeth more than the allotted fifteen minutes. I would not feel guilty for not brushing because I had no control over it.

After a few weeks, the toothbrushing was no longer a problem. There was really no explanation for this. I think it was simply a matter of "out of sight, out of mind.". . .

Focusing on Anorexia

How does everything I've been telling you about Westwood and the toothbrushing relate to the anorexia? Well, as you know, I'd been feeling fat for years, but never believed that I had the willpower to diet. Now, I saw that I did. The anorexia became the focus of my life.

I always believed that feeling fat was something I couldn't help. This was no longer the case. There was something I could do about it. I had the willpower to diet. I was all-powerful Michael. No longer would I feel fat and put up with it. Instead, I would do something or hate myself. Except for my family, Dr. B was the first person to whom I ever mentioned feeling fat. When I did this, he told me it was a characteristic of anorexia nervosa. "What's that?" I asked. When he explained the condition, I automatically labeled myself an anorexic. It's hard to explain, but it almost seemed "glamorous" to me (I don't know if that's the right word), something I wanted. I had an illness; I had something few others had; I was special. The anorexia gave me an identity and made me an individual.

It was at Westwood that I first became focused on the weight (number of pounds) itself. At one point, I was weighing myself hourly or every other hour. This did not last long. There was no point in constant weight checking. There would be basically no change.

The first way I noticed a difference in my weight was that my clothes felt loose. This made me feel *so* good. For the next five or six years, whenever I would be losing weight, I would get a "high" by getting dressed in the morning, and feeling that my pants had become that much bigger on me.

After being at Westwood for two months, my insurance ran out. There was really no reason for me not to go home. The toothbrushing wasn't a problem, and although I thought of losing weight, this had not yet become a serious issue. However, Dr. B and I did have one concern about my going home. It was mid-August, about three weeks before the start of school. We feared that in an unstructured environment, with a lot of free time on my hands, I would fall back into the habit of brushing my teeth. Because of this, it was decided that I would be transferred to the psychiatric ward of Norwood Hospital, a medical facility in Norwood, Massachusetts. (Insurance would not cover my stay at a private psychiatric hospital, but it would cover my stay on a psychiatric ward of a medical hospital.) I would stay there for about two weeks and go home one week before school started. This week would give me time to get back into the flow of everyday life outside the hospital.

In essence, Norwood was just "temporary housing" for me, noteworthy for only one reason. It was here that I had my first feelings of competition. There were one or two other anorexics (there had been none at Westwood). I felt that I had to be the skinniest, lose more weight than anyone else, and have the strictest guidelines around what I did or did not eat. These feelings were not strong, nor did I act on them. However, they were there.

Back to School

When I returned home from the hospital the last week in August 1984, I did not keep the anorexia a secret. When I had left school in April, I had said that it was because of mononucleosis. At the time, the other students knew that I studied a lot, but they did not know to what degree. The idea of seeing a psychiatrist, and later of being in a psychiatric hospital, had embarrassed me. I now knew that there was no reason for this embarrassment. Others could accept me as I was or shun me. It was their choice. . . .

Before my discharge from Westwood, Dr. B, my parents, and I had set a program I was to follow outside of the hospital. I needed to maintain my weight at 120 pounds, which was what it had been during my hospitalization. (I don't remember how much I had weighed before the hospital—maybe around 135.) Anything less would put me in serious medical danger and require rehospitalization, perhaps even tube feeding. This is a perfect example of why I now ignore doctors and believe that half the time, they don't know what they're talking about. Anything less than 120 pounds would be medically dangerous, and yet here I am today, not in great shape but functioning okay, at 75 pounds. . . .

On my first day back at school, I once again signed up for the cross-country track team. This would be my extracurricular activity. However, two days later, I quit. I was still depressed and just didn't have the motivation. Instead of a school-related activity, I got a part-time job. I worked approximately ten hours a week in the public library as a library page.

For the first few months of school, which were from September 1984 until the beginning of 1985, things remained basically the same. I was seeing [a new psychiatrist], Dr. P, two times a week and sticking to the agreement I had made upon leaving Westwood. Around the beginning of 1985, things began to go downhill.

My depression led to a lack of interest in socializing and other people. Soon, I had no friends and no social life. Some of my old friends remained faithful and let it be known that they would always be there for me, but I didn't really care.

I lost five pounds, going down to 115. . . .

Five Unusual Habits

In addition to the continuous depression, which had increased since my return to school, and the weight loss, I developed some unusual habits, which I still follow. The five most prevalent were (1) refusal to eat any low-calorie or diet foods, (2) refusal to let anyone see me eat, (3) constant wearing of jacket or bathrobes, (4) refusal to drink water, and (5) refusal to swallow my saliva.

(1) *Refusal to eat any low-calorie or diet foods.* I don't know if they are right, but this, along with the refusal to drink water, is a characteristic of mine that has led various therapists to label me as one of the most severe anorexics they have ever encountered. Many anorexics will allow themselves to fill up on low-calorie foods (diet sodas, salads, etc.), so that they will not be hungry. To me, this demonstrates a lack of willpower. I will not let myself fill up on these foods. Abstinence is the key to my feelings of self-control and being all-powerful almost as though restricting my intake is a challenge.

(2) *Refusal to let anyone see me eat.* Aside from my mother and brother, I will not eat in front of anyone. I first became uneasy in the school cafeteria. I felt that the other students were watching me, as if I were a pig. I started thinking, "Gee, they're probably wondering what I'm doing with food. After all, I have anorexia—I'm not supposed to eat." It was probably my imagination; they most likely never even noticed me. Odds are, none of them could have cared less. Still, I was uncomfortable and decided from then on to have my lunch in the bathroom, a private cubicle in the library, or anywhere else I wouldn't be seen. This carried over into my house. If we had guests, they did not see me eat.

(3) *Constant wearing of jacket or bathrobes.* Because I feel fat whenever I look at myself, I always wear a jacket in public to cover up my stomach. I don't mean occasionally, but almost all the time. When I am home, I will wear two bathrobes instead of the jacket, taking them off only when I go to bed or shower. I know that when I was in school, some of the students considered me strange because of my depression and unsociability. I don't know what they thought of my constant need to wear a jacket, but it probably added to my "weird" image. With one or two exceptions, since graduation, I haven't seen any of the kids from school. Maybe some of them are reading this book right now, thinking, "I remember that loser. So that's why he never took off his coat."

(4) *Refusal to drink water.* I do not drink water—I mean never. I have not had any water since February 1985. Now, I know there is water in everything. What I mean by no water is that I will not drink plain water; I will not go to a sink, pour myself some water, and drink it. This coincides with what I said earlier about my refusal to have any low-calorie or diet foods. The abstinence from water is almost like a challenge. I know water has no calories, but I would still feel fat if I drank it.

I remember the day I decided to stop drinking water. I had worked at the library from six in the evening until nine. I got home about fifteen minutes later, and ran to the sink to gulp down a few glasses of water. This was something I frequently did. With my dry mouth, a side effect of antidepressant medication and a result of limited intake, I was usually thirsty. After I had the water, I lifted my shirt, looked at my stomach, and felt so fat. I saw my stomach as sticking out, immensely bloated. I decided right then and there that I would never again drink water. If I was thirsty, that would be my tough luck. Talk about willpower. I have not had a drink of water since.

(5) *Refusal to swallow my saliva.* In March, a month after I stopped having water, I decided not to swallow my saliva. This is stupid, you say? I know. I agree. But, it's the way I am. I constantly spit out my saliva. To do this, I always have a paper cup or a paper towel in my jacket pocket. I spit into these twenty-four hours per day. Even when I go to sleep in the evening, I keep one or the other by my side.

False Hopes

Let me tell you a bit about Dr. P. Dr. B recommended him at the time of my discharge from Westwood Lodge. I saw Dr. P two times a week; each session lasted fifty minutes. For the first few months, I looked forward to our meetings. I wanted to get better and was willing to do anything. I guess I still thought of doctors as being miracle workers. This soon changed with Dr. P. . . .

What were our sessions like? Well, a typical session would start with each of us saying hello. Then we would sit down and look at each other. After doing this for fifty minutes, he would tell me that my time was up, and I would leave. This is the truth. I'm serious. He was getting paid around sixty dollars per hour, and we were staring at each other. That's all. No talking. I think I even occasionally dozed off (sixty dollars is an expensive nap).

In all, I saw Dr. P for almost two and a half years; our sessions came to an end when he moved to another state. During this time, my depression increased to the point where it could not get any worse. It never let up. I just wanted to die.

I frequently told my parents that I wanted to stop seeing Dr. P. He did not help and was a complete waste of time. I could be wrong, but I believe he was more interested in money than anything else (either that, or he was totally incompetent).

Because I felt that Dr. P was not helping, my parents sought the advice of Dr. B and other doctors whom they knew. However, all these doctors recommended that I continue to see Dr. P, and therefore, I did. Although I had become more depressed and lost a little weight, my parents did not know what else to do. Perhaps they feared that if I stopped seeing Dr. P, I would "fall apart." My parents were doing what they thought was best, maybe entertaining some false hope about what I could get out of these doctor appointments.

Males Are Anorexics, Too

Although concern about anorexia is growing, there is still a large unawareness, especially about male anorexia, and this is the major purpose of my story—so that other men with this problem will realize that they are not alone. My parents and I could not pick up a book and read about male anorexics. For all we knew, I was the only man in the world with anorexia. My parents did not know how to deal with me or even what to think. We had no one to whom we could turn. Perhaps if a book like this one had been around at the time, things would have been different.

KIRSTEN'S STORY: A NEED FOR UNCONDITIONAL LOVE AND SUPPORT

Peggy Claude-Pierre

Peggy Claude-Pierre is the founder of the Montreux Clinic in Victoria, Canada, which specializes in the treatment of eating disorders. In the following selection from her book *The Secret Language of Eating Disorders: The Revolutionary New Approach to Understanding and Curing Anorexia and Bulimia*, she describes her daughter Kirsten's struggle with anorexia and how it affected their lives. Out of this experience, explains Claude-Pierre, came her revelation that anorexia does not stem from concerns about looks or body image and is not specific to any age or gender. Anorexia, argues Claude-Pierre, is triggered by a negative mind-set that depresses a person so much that he or she perceives everything as "bad" or "wrong." She concludes that the most successful approach to combating anorexia is to treat the victim with patience and kindness fortified with unconditional love and support.

As a young woman, I was fortunate enough to have two incredible daughters. When they reached early adolescence, I resumed work toward an advanced degree in psychology at the university. I ended an incompatible marriage and moved to a new town to accelerate my studies, leaving behind a comfortable home for a small apartment. I had planned to have Kirsten, then fifteen, and Nicole, thirteen, join me, but Kirsten initially stayed behind to live with my parents and finish her school semester.

It was during those intervening months that Kirsten developed anorexia. One evening, my mother alerted me to the problem of my daughter's diminishing weight. Kirsten was studying until two or three in the morning, which was not unusual since she had always been a hardworking student. But my mother had noticed that Kirsten had large dark pools under her eyes, and she had lost a tremendous amount of weight in a short period of time. Hearing this, I asked Kirsten to join me.

When she walked off the plane, I was shocked to see that my daughter, who was five foot nine, now weighed less than a hundred pounds. She must have lost over twenty-five pounds while we had been apart. Going back to school was out of the question; she needed help—now. I told her, "Honey, you know you are staying with me."

She just looked back at me and said simply, "Yes, Mom, I know."

"What Did I Do Wrong?"

Under the surface, I was in a state of panic. I immediately look Kirsten to a doctor to check her electrolyte balance. He was the first in a procession of professionals. They all told me the same thing: Kirsten had anorexia and there was no cure for it. At best, an anorexic lived with it—that was called maintenance.

"How serious is it?" I asked. I knew the mortality rate was high. The doctor shook his head to indicate that Kirsten's prognosis was bleak.

I started reading everything I could about anorexia. I wanted to discover how I had failed this child. "What did I do wrong to make her hate herself so much?" I asked over and over again. Until I understood that, I would not know what the right help was. Everything I read told me that bad parenting, childhood trauma, sexual abuse, and a string of other "issues" were the cause.

Had our temporary separation caused Kirsten's illness? I felt remorse and extreme guilt. Naturally, as a single parent I assumed total blame for my daughter's illness, and the ensuing parade of psychiatrists did nothing to change my mind.

No Logical Sense

However, I balked at the psychiatrists' conclusion that Kirsten was being manipulative and selfish, that she was losing weight on purpose to get my attention. I had known this child all her life; I could not accept that she could change so radically from the kind, giving person I had always known her to be. Kirsten had always been unusually sensitive to and aware of other people's needs; in fact she was diligent about attending to them.

I asked my daughter to explain what she was thinking and feeling so I could understand how to help her. She told me that there seemed to be some other louder thought patterns in her head that made no logical sense. Yet Kirsten had always been a very logical child. It became obvious that she did not understand what was happening to her and was powerless to stop it. She said she felt she was going crazy. The medical doctors told me that she could not go on much longer in this manner.

I soon became aware that Kirsten felt terrible guilt about anything connected with food. Whenever I tried to persuade her to eat, she either refused, or tears would roll down her cheeks while she struggled to force the food down to please me. I remember taking her to a restaurant for a muffin. She ate it, but as we were leaving, I could tell she was feeling immense guilt about it. As we drove away I asked her, "Kirsten, I'm good enough for a muffin. What makes you think you're not good enough for a muffin?"

We stopped at a traffic light. She said, "Mom, see that light over there? You see that it's green. Logically, I know it's green, but my head tells me it's red, and I'm not allowed to go. That's the best analogy I can make for you about something that makes no sense to me. That's why I'm doing something so illogical."

She gave me similar clues about how her head operated. Later I realized that Kirsten's traffic-light analogy first made me understand that two minds were warring inside Kirsten's head. She was a determined person, and I kept trying to persuade her to fight against whatever force was barring her from eating in peace.

The Turning Point

The first two months were the most frightening. Occasionally at night, while Kirsten was sleeping, I would go quietly into her bedroom to check on her. Under her blankets, she was skeletal. I would slowly replace the blankets so she would not know I had been there, and she would not be concerned about my worry for her. It was hard to believe that she could survive; she was down to about eighty-four pounds. Fear almost paralyzed me.

She told me sadly one night, "Mom, you've never lied to me in your life, so I'm going to listen to you, even though the pressure is more than I can bear sometimes. Everything in me tells me not to trust anybody or anything at this point, but I've always trusted you. I'll continue to trust you, whatever it takes." To this day, I know that's what brought her through, and I stand in awe of her incredible courage against the unbelievable negativity of her mind.

In retrospect, I realize that her decision to trust me unconditionally was the turning point. She kept going to the doctors because I asked her to. Over the next six months, I worked with her every day. She even came to my university classes with me; I was loath to let her out of my sight. Intuitively I knew she should not be alone; otherwise this negativity, whatever it was, would gain strength in her mind when she was by herself.

After every meal, she would talk to me about the illogical thought patterns she could not get out of her head. She was direct about how she felt. Sometimes, she would look at some minuscule bit of food on her plate and tell me, "Mom, this hurts so much. I shouldn't be eating it. I should be eating a quarter of it. That's all I deserve." She felt almost subhuman, less than the rest of us. She never knew why she was less deserving, but she just knew she was.

In the first three or four months of her illness, Kirsten was suicidal and frightened, as if eating had some great negative consequence. I talked to her constantly. She was gentle, never abusive. Together we tried to work it out. For every illogical word or act, I responded gently with a logical discussion of the reality of the situation.

She cut off her hair and dyed it purple. At the time I did not pay much attention because I saw it as a natural consequence of being an adolescent. She dressed in layers as though she were trying to arm herself to fight the world; her natural gentleness began seeping away. It was as if she were on a search for self as she kept trying on different modes of appearance. She would wear outside what she seemed to lack inside for strength. (I would later learn that this is characteristic of many people with eating disorders.)

Since we had just moved to a new city, initially she no longer had any friends. I noticed that this normally outgoing girl did not even try to make new ones.

She became extremely agitated. She had to move all the time. If she needed to stay in one spot, she would walk in place; she could not sit in a chair without jiggling around excessively. She exercised all the time. I did not think that was such a problem, so I was not as on top of it as I might have been. Later I would know better.

An Unrelenting Nightmare

Several times Kirsten made statements that told me she perceived herself to be the adult in the situation, capable of making decisions that seemed rational to her but were anything but. At other times, she would say, "Mom, just let me go, just let me die. This is too hard; I can't fight it." I never heard, "Mom, help me." She never asked for help; I gave it to her, but she did not feel she was allowed to expect it.

She would never say that she was worried about me, but she was always trying to make life easier for me.

Then Kirsten started losing the ability to make any decisions, any choices at all; it was as if she had lost faith in her ability to choose. She second-guessed every possible decision or choice. When I asked about her preferences, she would respond, "Mom, what do you think?" "What will serve other people better?" She could not make the simplest choices about the most basic issues: what to wear, what restaurant to go to, what to eat. She was unable to create any of her own structure at all.

It was such an unrelenting nightmare. Not only was I terrified that my daughter was losing her life, but I was convinced I was the cause of her torment. Everywhere I went, I felt and accepted the stigma. The public knew that someone had to be blamed—the parent, the child, or both. I was overcome by the numbness of hopelessness. How could my child be dying in front of me? I knew I had to do something, but I did not know where to begin. The information I was getting made no sense. So little of it seemed to apply to Kirsten. Certainly, I would not accept that my daughter's anorexia was incurable. On occasion I glimpsed an idea that felt right, but essentially I felt terribly, terribly alone, left to stumble along an unfamiliar road in a strange country, whose signs were in a language I could not understand.

Search for an Answer

I found myself of two minds. On one hand, I was petrified that some-one could live with such agony—I was witnessing an emotional state that was unspeakably cruel on a continuous basis. On the other hand, I was irritated that I had allowed myself to see doctors as gods; I had expected physicians to have an answer for everything. Of course doc-tors are not wholly responsible for this deity complex; we put them on the pedestals ourselves. But how could I accept it when they told me my daughter was going to die, that she could never be cured? How could anybody give up on a psychological illness?

The doctors' explanations of Kirsten's illness were based on hap-penstance and theory, not on strict experience. I had so many ques-tions: Why does an eating disorder affect one child and not another in the same circumstance? I had read that most siblings of anorexics did not get the illness themselves. Did sexual abuse cause it? I knew that Kirsten had not been abused. Family trauma was another com-monly cited cause, but I knew that my daughter viewed my divorce as a positive event, not a traumatic one. I started searching for venues that would prove these issues to be the cause because I wanted desper-ately to find an answer that could reverse the consequences.

Never was I convinced that anorexia was primarily about weight. When Kirsten was sick, she expressed fears about getting fat, but it was not her main focus. She was much too composed to complain about her looks. She would tell me, "I need to be thinner. I don't know the reason why," and then she would start to cry

Given the public view that anorexia attacked adolescent girls, a group famously obsessed with looking right and fitting in, I assumed—wrongly—that Kirsten's illness was in part bound up with concerns about body image. I now know that anorexia does not depend on gen-der, age, or looks.

Unconditional Love and Support

I considered taking Kirsten to an eating disorders clinic. Every one that I investigated had a program based on behavior modification. The theory was that if you changed a person's actions, you would change the person. At these clinics, the therapists taught the patients that there were consequences to their behavior. They were given spe-cific goals, such as finishing a particular dish, and told that if they did not achieve the goal, there would be a consequence or punishment. They would be prohibited from seeing their parents, using the swim-ming pool, or engaging in some other enjoyable activity.

I felt intuitively that I had to separate Kirsten's actions from their consequences. My daughter was experiencing such intense punishment internally already that for me to inflict more would be counterproductive to her recovery. Logically, behavior modification did not seem reasonable, at least for this child.

For six months, I talked Kirsten through every meal and prepared all of them myself. At each meal, I would distract her with funny stories to take the onus off the fact that she was eating.

Kirsten's little sister, Nicole, was an enormous help; she did everything to please her sister. She spent every spare moment sitting with Kirsten, talking and joking with her, giving her things, trying to make a difference. Nicole became a completely selfless person during her sister's illness and stood by her with every possible fiber of her being. . . .

We combated Kirsten's illness with unconditional love and support. I refused to react to any rare bad behavior except with soothing statements like "I know you didn't mean to do that." I would never get angry under any circumstances. Intuitively I felt that something in Kirsten was testing me to find out how willing I was to be there for her. Kirsten was trying to let me know that she deserved nothing, but she was so gracious that the signals were not always apparent. It was a successful day if I just kept her alive.

Logic Is the Key

I was becoming more and more physically exhausted. I felt it was unsafe for me to sleep. What if something happened to Kirsten when my back was turned? I had tried to engage yet another specialist for insight, but he had neither the time nor the inclination. He was probably exhausted and disillusioned himself from the dearth of answers. "You're just one of many. I have no time," he told me, and I was devastated.

I felt that I was operating on base instinct. If I could only find the cause, then I would know how to reverse Kirsten's anorexia. I used to comfort myself with this thought, but in my more selfish moments, I longed for some respite. I lived in a void of uncertainty and desperation. The most lonely thought is that there must be an answer, but my daughter might die because I could not find it in time. I fought for my own sanity during this time as much as I did for Kirsten's.

Ultimately, it was Kirsten's incredibly logical, lawyer-like mind that helped bring her through. Anorexia knows no logic, and part of Kirsten's mind would insist repeatedly that she was not allowed to eat, or that she could subsist on some ridiculously small amount of food. I would argue her through it for hours, and she generously let me.

"Honey," I would attempt to reason with her, "what would you expect me to eat for a day?" I had to explain the logic of the situation every time. "Write down for me what you eat; would you be happy if I ate only that much?"

Later I realized that asking her to write out her daily menu may have been a mistake; I know now that in creating a written table of contents, the negative part of her mind could use it to reprimand her for her indulgence. (At some point in therapy, however, this can be a positive, even worthwhile interim structure.)

The Trigger Is Negativity

Slowly she became stronger. The dread drained from me as the days marched on and she became more confident. Eventually I realized she would make it, at least this time. But almost every book I had read warned me of the high rate of relapse, so I felt I could not really relax. My aim was not only to save her life, but to find out how to prevent a recurrence. What, then, was the trigger?

I began to suspect that relapse occurred when this negative mindset was somehow ignited; the trigger was something other than the anorexia itself. It seemed improbable that anorexia was a direct result of a single issue or even accumulated issues; perhaps it was the straw that broke the camel's back. Now I know: It is not the ten issues that finally become too much, but rather one's attitude toward and perception of the issues that brings on the manifestation of the condition. A person's negative mindset becomes increasingly pessimistic and subjective so that it searches out any issue to turn into another negative to feed itself. On its hunt for confirmation, it perverts any issue wherever it can because it is so hungry for negativity.

During that year, I continued to attend classes to become a psychologist and kept taking Kirsten with me. My field of interest was children. I was engaged in a major research project that involved twenty-six countries, studying how to prevent recidivism in juvenile delinquents released from prison. Two nations, Japan and Sweden, invited me to study with them for a year each. I was finding that kindness, not punishment, worked miracles. Later I would see this as a metaphor for my own work with victims of eating disorders.

It was another six months after Kirsten's weight had stabilized and the doctors declared her out of the woods that I could begin to feel safe about her. I know she suffered more than she ever told me. She has always had immense courage. Kirsten told me later that it took her almost another year after she had regained her weight to feel she had an assured self with internal guidelines that she could live with comfortably. Even though she was over the manifestation of her condition, she had needed that year to gain strength, to become as whole as every person ought to be.

CONTROLLED BY FOOD

Katie Street

In the following selection, Katie Street explains how she changed from a thin child and teenager into a very overweight college student. During this time, she admits, food totally controlled her. A compulsive overeater/binger, Street describes how her weight fluctuated from month to month because of her eating habits. Street confesses that although she was ashamed of her bingeing and went to great lengths to hide it, she could not control it. Street writes that her erratic eating—alternating between bingeing and dieting—affected not only her emotional well-being but her physical health and social life as well.

As a child, and up until I was a college freshman, I was thin. Active in many sports and recreational activities, I never thought about worrying how many calories are in a Snicker's candy bar, or the amount of fat grams in a pint of Ben & Jerry's raw cookie dough ice cream. Somehow, weight never caught up with me until I left home to start school in North Carolina.

I got lazy in college. I constantly drank beer. I can remember buying ham and bacon pizzas (my mouth is watering), a large—just for me. After gorging on pizza, I would empty the candy machine at 3 a.m. so no one would see me do it. I'd become so stuffed, I couldn't budge. Instead of the "freshman 15 (pounds)," I piled on the "freshman 50 and then some." By the end of the year, I was close to 200 pounds.

As a 25-year-old adult, I don't weigh close to that much anymore, but I do carry a load that feels heavy at times. I am a compulsive overeater/binger. My astrology sign is ideal for me—it's Libra (the scales). The scale can be my best friend or worst enemy. My compulsive obsessive behavior about food has affected my emotional well-being, physical health and social life.

An Obsession with Food

At one time, food entirely controlled me. It was always on my mind. I would sit in class in college and dream about chocolate mousse pie. I anticipated when I would eat next and what would it be. But, food

Reprinted from Katie Street, "Caloric Confessions," *American Fitness*, January/February 1998, by permission.

turned me into someone I didn't like. I remember weighing 175 pounds and feeling lousy.

I couldn't have just one cookie or scoop of ice cream. If I had one, it led to many. Sometimes I would get in my mind that I'd go on a food binge. My mind set itself in clockwork motion. I was on a mission to eat as much as I could all at once.

Once, when I was in college, I stopped at a Wendy's, McDonald's, gas station mart, Domino's pizza, Chinese restaurant and local grocery store. My roommate and I ate something at each stop. For some reason, once I began, it was almost impossible to stop. It was the fight on the inside that took me on an emotional roller coaster.

My weight fluctuated greatly. One month, I'd be skin and bones. The next, as big as a house. I am an expert at the Slim Fast, Weight Watchers, Diet Center, Nutri-System, Jenny Craig, Accutrim and Dynatrim diet plans. You name it, I've tried it. These diets are strenuous on the heart and body, not to mention getting those nasty stretch marks from yo-yo weight gain and loss.

I would go to bed at night anticipating weighing myself the next morning. In fact, I would weigh myself at least three times a day. It gave me power and a sense of control when I saw people stuffing themselves and refused even a bite. However, once I broke my diet, I could have been on a binge for a week, or even months, before I could get control again. I can remember one binge lasting from October until the middle of January. When I would stuff myself until it hurt, it would set off feelings of deep self-hatred.

I refused to eat like a horse in public, so I would go from place to place alone. I'd tell the waitress, "Oh, I'm starving. I haven't eaten all day!" The truth is it was probably my 12th dinner or 20th stop on a food binge. My friends and family wouldn't even know where I went, or why a whole box of Frosted Mini Wheat cereal was gone overnight.

Often, I would eat chocolate late at night when no one was watching. I could put away more chocolate than the Easter Bunny delivered. I would eat double chocolate fudge layer brownies with chocolate chips and triple chocolate icing. At one trip to Mrs. Field's Cookies, a friend and I bought some brownies. I downed five at a time without giving myself a chance to breathe. My friend only took a few bites and said, "Oh, I can't eat another bite. This is too rich." Too rich! I didn't know what that word meant. My chocolate affair ended when I went through a period of night sweats because I ate too much of it.

My long-term use of laxatives gave me one of the scariest episodes I've ever had in my life. I took two laxatives one afternoon and about 17 hours later, I felt my stomach walls scraping. This was usually a sign the laxatives kicked in. I was spending the night in a friend's dorm room, and walked into the bathroom to take a shower. As soon as I sat down on the toilet, hot and cold flashes swept over my entire body. I gripped the toilet paper holder because I felt dizzy. All of a sudden, I lost control of my bowels and was vomiting at the same time. When I had enough energy to run back to the room, my friend threw cold towels all over my body and stayed by my side until I felt better. After that day, I vowed never to take another laxative.

I also developed sharp pains in my esophagus. I found out it was because I didn't properly chew my food. When I ate, I'd shovel food in my mouth. For some reason, I felt like it was going to get up and run away from the plate. The pain got so bad, I'd fall to the floor and rock myself back and forth until it went away.

Of course, my problem affected my social life. If I didn't look right in my clothes, or my stomach was bulging out, I didn't want to go anywhere or do anything. I'd isolate myself from everyone around me. I didn't want anyone to look at me.

Taking Life One Day at a Time

I've grown in leaps and bounds from those days. I take life one day at a time. I wake up and walk two miles on my treadmill. I have a plan of what I will eat for the day that includes calories and fat. I also make sure I eat fruits and vegetables, along with a daily dose of skim milk. I have trained myself to portion out my food, so I don't eat a whole pizza myself. I keep all the good nutrients and vitamins in my body. I joke about the past because it helps me deal with it all.

Now, I make sure I work out daily and maintain my weight, which is a big feat for me. I wasted so much time beating myself up over my physical appearance. I just try to remember that even Ben & Jerry's raw cookie dough ice cream doesn't taste quite as good as looking healthy on the outside and, more importantly, the inside.

APPENDIX:

Physical Dangers of Eating Disorders

There are many men and women suffering with Anorexia or Bulimia who do not appear underweight—some may be of "average" weight, some may be slightly overweight. . . . Variations can be anywhere from extremely underweight to extremely overweight.

The outward appearance of an eating disorder victim does *not* dictate the amount of physical danger they are in, nor does it determine the emotional conflict they feel inside. Victims need not display even close to all of the below symptoms to be suffering.

A = Anorexia   B = Bulimia   C = Compulsive Overeating

● = Found in   √ = More common in   X = Does not apply

Physical Attribute or Danger	A	B	C
Starvation and Restriction of Food—calories and/or fat grams sometimes accompanied by self-induced vomiting, laxatives, diuretics, or obsessive exercise with any food intake, or without food intake at all.	●	X	X
Binge and Purge Episodes—abnormally large intake of food followed by self-induced vomiting, intake of laxatives or diuretics, obsessive exercise, and/or periods of starvation.	X	●	X
Overeating. Binge Episodes—abnormally large, uncontrollable intake of food.	X	X	●
Malnutrition—caused by undereating or overeating. The word malnutrition indicates deficiency of energy, protein, and micronutrients (e.g., vitamin A, iodine, and iron) either singularly or in combination. It can cause severe health risks including (but not limited to) respiratory infections, kidney failure, blindness, heart attack, and death.	√	√	●
Dehydration—caused by the depletion or lack of intake of fluids in the body. Restriction/starvation, vomiting, and laxative abuse are the primary causes in victims of eating disorders. Symptoms include dizziness, weakness, or darkening of urine. It can lead to kidney failure, heart failure, and death.	●	●	X
Electrolyte Imbalances—electrolytes are essential to the production of the body's "natural electricity" that ensures healthy teeth, joints and bones, nerve and muscle impulses, kidneys and heart, blood sugar levels, and the delivery of			

Physical Attribute or Danger	A	B	C
oxygen to the cells.	√	√	•
Vitamin and Mineral Deficiencies	•	•	•
Lanugo—soft downy hair on face, back and arms. This is caused due to a protective mechanism built into the body to help keep a person warm during periods of starvation and malnutrition and the hormonal imbalances that result.	√	•	X
Edema—swelling of the soft tissues as a result of excess water accumulation. It is most common in the legs and feet of Compulsive Overeaters and in the abdominal area of Anorexics and/or Bulimics (can be caused by laxative and diuretic use).	√	•	•
Muscle Atrophy—wasting away of muscle and decrease in muscle mass due to the body feeding off of itself.			
Impaired Neuromuscular Function—due to vitamin and mineral deficiencies (specifically potassium) and malnutrition.	√	•	X
Insomnia—having problems falling and/or staying asleep.			
Chronic Fatigue Syndrome—continuous and crippling fatigue related to a weakened immune system.			
Hyperactivity—manic bouts of not being able to sit still.	•	•	•
Swelling—in face and cheeks (following self-induced vomiting).	•	√	X
Callused or Bruised Fingers—this is caused by repeatedly using the fingers to induce vomiting.	•	√	X
Tearing of Esophagus—caused by self-induced vomiting.			
Mallory-Weiss Tear—associated with vomiting; a tear of the gastroesophageal junction.			
Gastric Rupture—spontaneous stomach erosion, perforation, or rupture.	•	√	X
Esophageal Reflux (Acid Reflux Disorders)—partially digested items in the stomach, mixed with acid and enzymes, regurgitate back into the esophagus. This can lead to damage to the esophagus, larynx, and lungs and increases the chances of developing cancer of the esophagus and voice box.			
Barrett's Esophagus—associated with cancer of the esophagus and caused by esophageal reflux, this is a change in the cells within the esophagus.	•	√	•
Cancer—of the throat and voice box (larynx) due to acid reflux disorders.	•	√	X
Dry Skin and Hair, Brittle Hair and Nails, Hair Loss—caused			

Physical Attribute or Danger	A	B	C
by Vitamin and Mineral deficiencies, malnutrition, and dehydration.	•	•	X
Low Blood Pressure, Hypotension—caused by lowered body temperature, malnutrition, and dehydration. Can cause heart arrhythmias, shock, or myocardial infarction. *Orthostatic Hypotension*—sudden drop in blood pressure upon sitting up or standing. Symptoms include dizziness, blurred vision, passing out, heart pounding, and headaches.	•	•	X
High Blood Pressure, Hypertension—elevated blood pressure exceeding 140 over 90. Can cause blood vessel changes in the back of the eye, creating vision impairment; abnormal thickening of the heart muscle; kidney failure; and brain damage.	X	X	•
Disruptions in Blood Sugar Levels: —Low Blood Sugar/Hypoglycemia—can indicate problems with the liver or kidneys and can lead to neurological and mental deterioration. —Elevated Blood Sugar/Hyperglycemia—can lead to diabetes, liver, and kidney shutdown, circulatory and immune system problems.	•	•	•
Diabetes—high blood sugar as a result of low production of insulin. This can be caused by hormonal imbalances, hyperglycemia, or chronic pancreatitis.	•	•	√
Iron Deficiency, Anemia—this makes the oxygen-transporting units within the blood useless and can lead to fatigue, shortness of breath, increased infections, and heart palpitations.	•	•	X
Kidney Infection and Failure—your kidneys "clean" the poisons from your body, regulate acid concentration, and maintain water balance. Vitamin deficiencies, dehydration, infection, and low blood pressure increase the risks of and are associated with kidney infection, thus making permanent kidney damage and kidney failure more likely.	•	•	•

Osteoporosis—thinning of the bones with reduction in bone mass due to depletion of calcium and bone protein, predisposing to fractures.

Osteopenia—below-normal bone mass indicating a calcium and/or vitamin D deficiency and leading to Osteoporosis. (Hormone imbalance/deficiencies associated with the loss of the menstrual cycle can also increase your risks of Osteoporosis and Osteopenia.)

Physical Attribute or Danger	A	B	C
Arthritis (degenerative)—can be caused by hormonal imbalances and vitamin deficiencies as well as increased stress on the joints in individuals who are suffering Compulsive Overeating.	●	●	●
TMJ "Syndrome" and Related TMJ Problems—degenerative arthritis within the tempero-mandibular joint in the jaw (where the lower jaw hinges to the skull) creating pain in the joint area, headaches, and problems chewing and opening/closing the mouth. Vitamin deficiencies and teeth grinding (often related to stress) can both be causes.	●	●	X
Amenorrhea—loss of menstrual cycle (due to lack of secreting hormone, oestrogen, by the ovaries). Loss of the menstrual cycle can also lead to Osteopenia and Osteoporosis.	●	●	●
Easily Bruising Skin—vitamin deficiencies that decrease the body's ability to heal itself, low blood pressure, and extreme weight loss will all lead to easily bruised skin that can take a long time to heal.	√	●	X
Dental Problems, Decalcification of Teeth, Erosion of Tooth Enamel, Severe Decay, Gum Disease—will be caused by stomach acids and enzymes (from vomiting); vitamin D and calcium deficiencies, and hormonal imbalance. Can also be due to the lack of exercise the teeth can get from the process of eating certain foods. Dental problems can sometime indicate problems with the heart.	√	√	●
Liver Failure—the liver aids in removing waste from cells and aids in digestion. You cannot live without your liver. Fasting and taking acetaminophen (drug found in over-the-counter pain killers) increases your risk of liver damage and failure. Loss of menstruation and dehydration (putting women at risk for too much iron in their system) and chronic heart failure can lead to liver damage or failure.	●	●	●

Bad Circulation, Slowed or Irregular Heartbeat, Arrhythmias, Angina, Heart Attack—there are many factors associated with having an eating disorder that can lead to heart problems or a heart attack. Sudden cardiac arrest can cause permanent damage to the heart or instant death. Anorexia/Bulimia: electrolyte imbalances (especially potassium deficiency), dehydration, malnutrition, low blood pressure, extreme orthostatic hypotension, abnormally slow heart rate, and hormonal imbalances can all cause serious problems with the heart.

Compulsive Overeating: high blood pressure, accumulation

Physical Attribute or Danger	A	B	C
of fat deposits around the heart muscle, high cholesterol, decreased exercise due to lack of mobility, diabetes, and hormonal imbalances can all lead to serious problems with the heart.	•	•	•
Infertility—the inability to have children. Caused by loss of menstrual cycle and hormonal imbalances. Malnutrition and vitamin deficiencies can also make it impossible to succeed with a full-term pregnancy and can increase the chances significantly of a baby born with birth defects.	•	•	•
Problems During Pregnancy—including potential for high risk pregnancies, miscarriage, stillborn babies and death or chronic illness, from minor to severe, in children born (all due to malnutrition, dehydration, vitamin and hormone deficiencies).	•	•	•
Depression—mood swings and depression will all be caused by physiological factors such as electrolyte imbalances, hormone and vitamin deficiencies, malnutrition, and dehydration. Living with the eating disorder behaviors themselves will cause depression. Depression can also lead the victim back into the cycle of the eating disorder (or may have initially been the problem before the onset of the eating disorder). Stress within family, job, and relationships can all be causes. There are also a percentage of people born with a pre-disposition to depression, based on family history. Can lead to suicide.	•	•	•
Lowered Body Temperature (Temperature Sensitivity)—caused by loss of healthy insulating layer of fat and lowered blood pressure.	•	•	X
Cramps, Bloating, Constipation, Diarrhea, Incontinence—increased or decreased bowel activity.	•	•	•
Peptic Ulcers—caused by increased stomach acids, cigarette smoking, high consumption of caffeine or alcohol.			
Pancreatitis—this is when the digestive enzymes attack the pancreas. It can be caused by repeated stomach trauma (such as with vomiting), alcohol consumption, or the excessive use of laxatives or diet pills.	•	√	•
Digestive Difficulties—a deficiency in digestive enzymes will lead to the body's inability to properly digest food and absorb nutrients. This can lead to malabsorption problems, malnutrition, and electrolyte imbalances.	•	•	X
Weakness and Fatigue—caused by generalized poor eating			

Physical Attribute or Danger	A	B	C
habits, electrolyte imbalances, vitamin and mineral deficiencies, depression, malnutrition, heart problems.	•	•	•
Seizures—the increased risk of seizures in Anorexic and Bulimic individuals may be caused by dehydration. It is also possible that lesions on the brain caused by long-term malnutrition and lack of oxygen-carrying cells to the brain may play a role.	√	•	X
Death caused by any of the following or any combination of the following: heart attack or heart failure, lung collapse, internal bleeding, stroke, kidney failure, liver failure, pancreatitis, gastric rupture, perforated ulcer, depression, and suicide.	•	•	•

Amy Medina, "Physical Dangers," 1998. On-Line. Something Fishy Website on Eating Disorders. Internet. Available www.something-fishy.com.

Organizations to Contact

The editors have compiled the following list of organizations concerned with the issues debated in this book. The descriptions are derived from materials provided by the organizations. All have publications or information available for interested readers. The list was compiled on the date of publication of the present volume; the information provided here may change. Be aware that many organizations take several weeks or longer to respond to inquiries, so allow as much time as possible.

American Anorexia/Bulimia Association, Inc. (AA/BA)
165 W. 46th St., #1108, New York, NY 10036
(212) 575-6200
e-mail: amanbu@aol.com • web address: http://members.aol.com/amanbu

AA/BA is a nonprofit organization that works to prevent eating disorders by informing the public about their prevalence, early warning signs, and symptoms. AA/BA also provides information about effective treatments to sufferers and their families and friends.

American Psychiatric Association (APA)
1400 K St. NW, Washington, DC 20005
(202) 682-6000 • fax: (202) 682-6850
e-mail: apa@psych.org • web address: http://www.psych.org

APA is an organization of psychiatrists dedicated to studying the nature, treatment, and prevention of mental disorders. It helps create mental health policies, distributes information about psychiatry, and promotes psychiatric research and education. APA publishes the monthly *American Journal of Psychiatry*.

American Psychological Association
750 First St. NE, Washington, DC 20002-4242
(202) 336-5500 • fax: (202) 336-5708
e-mail: public.affairs@apa.org
web address: http://www.apa.org

This society of psychologists aims to "advance psychology as a science, as a profession, and as a means of promoting human welfare." It produces numerous publications, including the monthly journal *American Psychologist*, the monthly newspaper *APA Monitor*, and the quarterly *Journal of Abnormal Psychology*.

Anorexia Nervosa and Bulimia Association (ANAB)
767 Bayridge Dr., PO Box 20058, Kingston, ON K7P 1CO, CANADA
web address: http://www.ams.queensu.ca/anab/

ANAB is a nonprofit organization made up of health professionals, volunteers, and past and present victims of eating disorders and their families and friends. The organization advocates and coordinates support for individuals affected directly or indirectly by eating disorders. As part of its effort to offer a broad range of current information, opinion, and/or advice concerning eating disorders, body image, and related issues, ANAB produces the quarterly newsletter *Reflections*.

Anorexia Nervosa and Related Eating Disorders, Inc. (ANRED)
PO Box 5102, Eugene, OR 97405
(503) 344-1144
web address: http://www.anred.com

ANRED is a nonprofit organization that provides information about anorexia
nervosa, bulimia nervosa, binge eating disorder, compulsive exercising, and
other lesser-known food and weight disorders, including details about recovery
and prevention. ANRED offers workshops, individual and professional
training, as well as local community education. It also produces a monthly
newsletter.

Eating Disorders Awareness and Prevention, Inc. (EDAP)
603 Stewart St., Suite 803, Seattle, WA 98101
(206) 382-3587 • fax: (206) 292-9890
web address: http://members.aol.com/edapinc

EDAP is dedicated to promoting the awareness and prevention of eating disorders
by encouraging positive self-esteem and size acceptance. It provides free
and low-cost educational information on eating disorders and their prevention.
EDAP also provides educational outreach programs and training for
schools and universities and sponsors the Puppet Project for Schools and the
annual National Eating Disorders Awareness Week. EDAP publishes a prevention
curriculum for grades four through six as well as public prevention and
awareness information packets, videos, guides, and other materials.

Food Addicts Anonymous (FAA)
4623 Forest Hill Blvd., Suite 109-4, West Palm Beach, FL 33415-9120
(561) 967-3871
web address: http://www.erols.com/randrc/faa

FAA is a fellowship of men and women recovering from food addiction.
Through a twelve-step program based on the belief that food addiction is a
biochemical disease, its members work to stay abstinent and help other food
addicts achieve abstinence. FAA publishes a quarterly newsletter and the book
Food Addiction, the Body Knows.

Harvard Eating Disorders Center (HEDC)
356 Boylston St., Boston, MA 02118
(888) 236-1188

HEDC is a national nonprofit organization dedicated to research and education.
It works to expand knowledge about eating disorders and their detection,
treatment, and prevention and promotes the healthy development of
women, children, and everyone at risk. A primary goal for the organization
is lobbying for health policy initiatives on behalf of individuals with eating
disorders.

National Association of Anorexia and Associated Disorders (ANAD)
Box 7, Highland Park, IL 60035
(847) 831-3438 • hot line: (847) 831-3438 • fax: (847) 433-4632
e-mail: anad20@aol.com • web address: http://members.aol.com/anad20/

ANAD offers hot-line counseling, operates an international network of support
groups for people with eating disorders and their families, and provides
referrals to health care professionals who treat eating disorders. It produces a
quarterly newsletter and information packets and organizes national conferences
and local programs. All ANAD services are provided free of charge.

National Eating Disorder Information Centre (NEDIC)
CW 1–211, 200 Elizabeth St., Toronto, ON M5G 2C4, CANADA
(416) 340-4156 • fax: (416) 340-4736
e-mail: mbeck@torhosp.toronto.on.ca • web address: http://www.nedic.on.ca
NEDIC provides information and resources on eating disorders and weight preoccupation, and it focuses on the socio-cultural factors that influence female health-related behaviors. NEDIC promotes healthy lifestyles and encourages individuals to make informed choices based on accurate information. It publishes a newsletter and a guide for families and friends of eating-disorder sufferers and sponsors Eating Disorders Awareness Week in Canada.

National Eating Disorders Organization (NEDO)
6655 S. Yale Avenue, Tulsa, OK 74136
(918) 481-4044
web address: http://www.laureate.com
NEDO provides information, prevention, and treatment resources for all forms of eating disorders. It believes that eating disorders are multidimensional, developed and sustained by biological, social, psychological, and familial factors. It publishes information packets, a video, and a newsletter, and it holds a semiannual national conference.

Overeaters Anonymous (OA)
6075 Zenith Ct. NE, Rio Rancho, NM 87124
(505) 891-2664 • fax: (505) 891-4320
web address: http://www.overeatersanonymous.org
OA is a fellowship of individuals recovering from compulsive overeating. OA's main purpose is to abstain from compulsive overeating and help others who suffer from the disorder. The organization offers a recovery program and publishes *Lifeline,* a monthly magazine.

Weight-Control Information Network (WIN)
1 WIN Way, Bethesda, MD 20892-3665
(800) WIN-8098 • (301) 984-7378 • fax: (301) 984-7196
e-mail: win@info.niddk.nih.gov • web address: http://www.niddk.nih.gov
WIN is a service of the National Institute of Diabetes and Digestive and Kidney Diseases at the National Institutes of Health. It assembles and distributes science-based information on weight control, obesity, and nutritional disorders. WIN produces videos in its Clinical Nutrition and Obesity lecture series and a quarterly newsletter for health professionals, *WIN Notes.*

BIBLIOGRAPHY

Books

Suzanne Abraham and Derek Llewellyn-Jones	*Eating Disorders: The Facts.* Oxford, England: Oxford University Press, 1997.
Jean Antonello	*Breaking Out of Food Jail: How to Free Yourself from Diets and Problem Eating Once and For All.* New York: Simon & Schuster, 1996.
Frances M. Berg	*Afraid to Eat: Children and Teens in Weight Crisis.* Hettinger, ND: Healthy Weight Journal, 1997.
Peggy Claude-Pierre	*The Secret Language of Eating Disorders: The Revolutionary New Approach to Understanding and Curing Anorexia and Bulimia.* New York: Times Books, 1997.
Carolyn Costin	*Your Dieting Daughter: Is She Dying for Attention?* New York: Brunner/Mazel, 1997.
Viola Fodor	*Desperately Seeking Self: An Inner Guidebook for People with Eating Problems.* Carlsbad, CA: Gurze Books, 1997.
Nan Kathryn Fuchs	*Overcoming the Legacy of Overeating: How to Change Your Negative Eating Habits.* Los Angeles: Lowell House, 1996.
Michael Fumento	*The Fat of the Land: The Obesity Epidemic and How Overweight Americans Can Help Themselves.* New York: Viking, 1997.
Rosemary Green	*Diary of a Fat Housewife.* New York: Warner Books, 1996.
Sharlene Janice Hesse-Biber	*Am I Thin Enough Yet? The Cult of Thinness and the Commercialization of Identity.* New York: Oxford University Press, 1996.
Marya Hornbacher	*Wasted: A Memoir of Anorexia and Bulimia.* New York: HarpersFlamingo, 1998.
Anne Katherine	*Anatomy of a Food Addiction: The Brain Chemistry of Overeating: An Effective Program to Overcome Compulsive Eating.* Carlsbad, CA: Gurze Books, 1996.
Michael Krasnow	*My Life as a Male Anorexic.* New York: Harrington Park Press, 1996.
Steven Levenkron	*Treating and Overcoming Anorexia Nervosa.* New York: Warner Books, 1997.
Michelle Joy Levine	*I Wish I Were Thin, I Wish I Were Fat: The Real Reasons We Overeat and What We Can Do About It.* Huntington Station, NY: Vanderbilt Press, 1997.
Susie Orbach	*Fat Is a Feminist Issue: The Anti-Diet Guide for Women.* New York: Galahad Books, 1997.
Mary Bray Pipher	*Hunger Pains: The Modern Woman's Tragic Quest for Thinness.* New York: Ballantine Books, 1997.

Dierdra Price   *Healing the Hungry Self: The Diet-Free Solution to Lifelong Weight Management.* New York: Plume, 1998.

Kathryn J. Zerbe *The Body Betrayed: A Deeper Understanding of Women, Eating Disorders, and Treatment.* Carlsbad, CA: Gurze Books, 1995.

Periodicals

Arla Amara and Paul L. Cerrato "Eating Disorders—Still a Threat," *RN,* June 1996. Available from 5 Paragon Dr., Montvale, NJ 07645-1735.

Barbara Apgar "D-fenfluramine Therapy for Binge Eating Disorder," *American Family Physician,* May 1, 1997. Available from 8880 Ward Parkway, Kansas City, MO 64114-2762.

Liz Applegate "Running into Trouble," *Runner's World,* April 1998.

Behavioral Health Treatment "Eating Disorders Still Confound Experts: Field Has No Magic Bullet for Treatment," June 1997.

Liz Brody   "On the Dark Side," *Shape,* March 1997. Available from 21100 Erwin Street, Woodland Hills, CA 91367-3712.

Business Week "Is There a Cure for Obesity?" February 8, 1998.

Shannon Dortch "America Weighs In," *American Demographics,* June 1997.

Carey Goldberg "Surgery Offers Hope, Risks for Obese People," *New York Times,* January 1, 1997.

Denise Grady "Efforts to Fight Eating Disorders May Backfire," *New York Times,* May 7, 1997.

JAMA   "Long-Term Pharmacotherapy in the Management of Obesity," December 18, 1996. Available from 515 N. State St., Chicago, IL 60610.

Caroline Knapp "Body Language: Are People with Eating Disorders Desperate for Control or Just Too Sensitive for Their Own Good?" *New York Times Book Review,* January 4, 1998.

Carol Krucoff "Is Your Child Dying to Win?" *Washington Post,* March 3, 1998. Available from 1150 15th St. NW, Washington, DC, 20071.

Robert Langreth "Eminent Journal Urges Moratorium on Diet-Drug Use," *Wall Street Journal,* August 28, 1997.

Richard A. Marini "Bingeing to Feel Nothing," *Weight Watchers Magazine,* September/October 1997. Available from 2100 Lakeshore Dr., Birmingham, AL 35209-6721.

Tracy Nesdoly "The First Bite: Kids' Eating Disorders Are a Serious Concern," *Maclean's,* June 17, 1996.

Susan Okie   "Anorexia May Depend in Part on Genes," *Washington Post,* January 27, 1998.

Christine F. Ridout	"Glutton for Punishment: Binge Eaters Are Impulsive and Often Unable to Control Their Emotions and Behavior," *American Fitness*, November/December 1997. Available from 15250 Ventura Blvd, Suite 200, Sherman Oaks, CA 91403-3215.
Suzanne Schlosberg	"Fear and Loathing of Food," *Shape*, March 1998.
Betsy Streisand	"Overcoming Anorexia: Peggy Claude-Pierre's Controversial Eating-Disorder Cure," *U.S. News & World Report*, September 29, 1997.
Mackenzie Stroh and John Searles	"Anorexia: Eating Disorder Investigation," *Cosmopolitan*, October 1997. Available from 1224 W. 57th Street, New York, NY 10019-3212.
Leslie Vreeland	"Dying to Be Thin—After 30,"*Good Housekeeping*, March 1998.
Dorine Wilson and Micki Siegel	"My Daughter's Dangerous Obsession," *Good Housekeeping*, March 1997.

INDEX